WENDY POTEAT-SPICER

OWN YOUR TRUTH

*"LIVING LIFE ACCORDING TO YOUR
OWN TRUTH AND YOUR OWN TERMS"*

Published by Lee's Press and Publishing Company

www.LeesPress.net

ISBN-13: 978-0999310359 *Paperback*

ISBN-10: 0999310356

Table of Contents

Acknowledgements

When I began writing this book, Timothy Spicer was my fiancé. On May 26, 2017 he became my husband. Our wedding was the most beautiful day of my life. The low country provided a magical backdrop as we exchanged vows by the Stono River, in front of over 200 of our closets family members and friends. I acknowledge him for being my biggest fan. No matter what I'm going through he is there to be my best friend and help me through. Although people didn't believe that our love was genuine, we knew what work God had done in our lives and knew that our love would stand the test of time. Timothy, I love you and thank you for loving me unconditionally and showing me what real love feels like. Thank you for allowing me to share your sons. T.J., the oldest of our 6 boys, is the true definition of focused. He knows how to have fun too. However, he is so directed in the path that he is taking with his life. It warms my heart to hear him talk about graduate school knowing he will one day be a major impact player in the world of education. Devin, your middle son, lives out the definition of the moody and embattled middle child, but we both know that he is brilliant and will find his way. I love him in spite of him having a hard time expressing his love for us both. Jalen had my heart before we even knew each other. It has been a true blessing watching him grow into a fine young man. He begins his journey this fall as a college basketball player for NC A&T, following in your footsteps. A good friend's mother once told me that love does not hurt you intentionally and when it does run. I am thankful that I have finally been blessed with a love that I never have any intention of running from.

Many thanks to Viveca Wingfield for always pushing me to be a better person even when the devil was working to make me do the wrong thing. For years I avoided you because you reminded me so much of my own mother. Once we finally got a chance to get to know each other, I realized that God put you in my life to be the mother that I needed. Always being the voice of reason to reel me back in. I am honored to say that I have you in my life to encourage me and praise me on my successes. I could not have asked for a better person to stand in the gap for me. I love you to the moon and back. God knew exactly when I would be able to accept the love you would give. I am so thankful God gave me you to call mama.

Joy Cook is the first person that I shared my story with and verbalized that I was ready to tell the story to help others. She said something to me that stuck with me for many years, as I prepared myself to tell my story, which I will never forget. Joy said that I was meant to be a star and my story would change lives. Thank you for believing in me and my dream, even when I wasn't sure of it myself. Thank you for saying this one line at your Big Hat Brunch…"Done is better than perfect!" You are a true inspiration and gave me the last push I needed to put pen to paper and create this book.

Dedication

I dedicate this book to my beautiful mother, Dorothy Robinson Poteat. I had her with me on earth for 19 years, and she was my best friend, my comforter and my rock. I watched her suffer for so many years with abuse and depression that it was normal to me. When I lost her, there was a void left in my heart and in my soul that has never been filled. I dedicate this book to her as my way of giving her the voice that she never had. My wish is that by sharing my story that I will also give power to the struggle that she endured.

My two youngest sons have saved my life many times and never even knew it. There were many times on my journey that I wanted to give up and the mere sound of their voices picked me up and carried me on. William "Tre'" Turner, you make being a parent an easy job. Thank you for your God filled spirit and your great big heart. Thank you for making sure I am always ok when you can see that I am down. I love you my Dooga! Walter Turner is my baby boy, and you take the "baby" position to a whole different level. Thank you for being the definition of a mama's boy. You are so full of laughter, talent, and love that it absolutely exudes from you. Never change who you are and continue to sing with that beautiful voice that you get from your mama. I love you Walty! I dedicate my truth to you both!

I also dedicate this book to my oldest son PJ Hairston. I gave birth to him on Christmas Eve in 1992 at a time in my life when I was at my lowest. He was my gift from God to save my life, and for that, I am eternally grateful to the little boy with big brown eyes that started my process of healing. I hope that you read this book and are inspired to do the same thing with your story. You are powerful and a leader. You have been ordained by God with your own story, and I pray you will be led to put pen to paper.

Introduction

Owning your truth is one of the hardest steps in moving forward into your purpose. To look at yourself with full accountability for everything, the good and the bad, is a self-reflecting step that has transformative value. To accept what you have been through as a lesson and blessing allows you to free yourself from anger and blame. As you read this book allow yourself to take a pause and process what you have read. Allow yourself to shed tears as your own story is connected to the words. Allow yourself to question what is next for you in your life. Allow yourself to understand the true meaning of owning your truth.

This book is my account of many different things that have happened over the course of my life. Revealing intimate details in the following pages was not easy, but it was necessary. In order to move into the next phases of my life with transparency the details are necessary, I often time say in my work life and my personal life, partnerships move at the speed of trust. I have written this book to build a relationship with my readers. This book shares with others my "why" for the way I live my life. It is also intended to begin building the trust and bond that I want to create with each reader.

Please read through the 6 steps included very carefully, The steps transformed the way I live my life and I believe it can do the same for each reader. They are not complicated steps however, they are not simple steps either. The commitment and self-awareness needed to use the steps is an individual choice, but I believe if the effort is made it will change your life. It is intentional that I am very candid in telling my story in hopes that it will resonate to someone and help someone through whatever struggle is holding them captive. There is nothing worse than being in a state of stuck.

Foreword

When I was asked to write the foreword to this book, I must admit I was dumbfounded. I am not a writer was my first thought, but then the author explained to me what the foreword was and why she wanted me to write it. I said yes, but still felt angst about writing. I am what the author calls a celebrity and as she puts it a bit infamous as well. My name is Samuel Peterson Hairston Jr. aka "PJ". My claim to fame is the ability to play basketball and as the author said my ability to stay on the ESPN ticker. I played basketball for Coach Roy Williams at the University of North Carolina for 2 seasons. I was never back on the court after the second season for some mistakes that I made as an impressionable 19-20-year-old, who thought that I ruled the world. I was the first player to be in college and then the next semester playing in the D-League, which is where I landed, with the Texas Legends, when I was not allowed to remain on the basketball team. I was drafted in the first round of the 2014 NBA Draft, becoming the first D-League player to ever be drafted in the first round of the NBA draft. I played 2 years for the Charlotte Hornets. My 3rd year option on my contract was not picked up and I was traded right after the all-star break to the Memphis Grizzlies. I was not offered a contract to come back to the Grizzlies and entered the off season of 2016 as an unrestricted free agent. My reputation for not being a mature professional hindered me from finding a team and one bad mistake, of not making a workout, caused me to not be signed until late in the 2016 by the Houston Rockets.

Houston sent me to the D-League and retained my rights. I was injured and to be honest angry that I was back in the D-League and I squandered the opportunity to make the roster for the Rockets during the season. I became out of shape and injury prone and ended up back home. I took some time to get my mind and my body right. I rehabbed and now I'm currently focused on getting back into NBA player shape and determined that I will be a contributor to a team during the 2017-2018 season.

The author of this book is someone that I have known my entire life. She is the one person that has always supported me. She is also the one person that is so brutally honest that it hits you over the head like a ton of bricks. I'm sure that anyone that googles my name can read the media accounts of my issues at UNC, but this woman lived it. She lived through the scrutiny and social media attacks. She dealt with the constant barrage of media that camped out by her home. She lived with watching my name on the ESPN ticker for an entire summer. She lived with the hurt, which I'm sure brought her to tears on many nights. To be honest, UNC was not the only time this woman had to live through me being in the news. I have not been the easiest person to stand by and in this foreword, I want to say to this woman; I am sorry for all the things that I have put you though and thank you of never giving up on me, even when I had given up on myself.

The author of this book, Wendy K. Poteat-Spicer gave me life and I am very proud to say that my mommy is my hero! Her life journey is nothing short of amazing! This book is not just about, what I'm sure she sees as a never-ending saga with me, her oldest son. This book is about the hurt that you can experience from family. It is about domestic violence. It is about drug abuse, alcoholism, and self-medication to deal with depression. It is a full account of the extraordinary life that my mom has lived and the triumph she lives today. I know everyone wants to know the details about what happened at UNC too; well she gives you her full account of what she went through and not what the media reported. This book is about transparency and owning your own mess to come out on top. My mother is a true testament that all the bad things that happen in life do not have to consume you and it does not dictate your future. This book tells you in very specific ways how to turn your life around and take control of your own destiny. After reading this book I understand why she is so matter of fact and I also have a better understanding of what steps I need to make in my own life to build a better future for myself and my daughter.

I am writing this foreword because I believe in my mom. I believe that God has given her a special gift to change lives. I am also writing this foreword because my mom made me realize that I have a story to tell and this foreword is the spring board to my own book. I am still a work in progress, but one thing is for sure. My mom, the author of this book, will always be my biggest supporter and my biggest critic. Hopefully this book will push you to some hard truths just as it has pushed me. Time for everyone to *OWN YOUR TRUTH*!

Samuel Peterson Hairston, Jr. "PJ"

Chapter 1

My First Experience

The sound of arguing is getting louder and louder. I can hear my mom screaming and crying for him to stop. I am in my safe place rocking back and forth with tears streaming down my cheeks. I can taste the saltiness as the front of my shirt is soaked with the wetness of my tears. I hear the dishes breaking and then it just stopped. I was scared, but I had to see if my mom was ok. I ran into the kitchen, and she was sitting on the floor, and her hands were covered in blood. As I ran towards her, a plate hit me across my hand and I see blood running down my hand. My dad screamed at me to get my stupid ass out of the way and go back to my room. His face looked so mean. My mom grabbed me and shuffled back to my bedroom. She told me to stay there as she walked back up the hallway. I crawled into my closet and listened to things break and yelling for what seemed like hours. Domestic violence and crying in a closet are my first childhood memories. My first experience would definitely not be my last.

I grew up on Burton's Chapel Rd in a little place called Sweet Gum, named after all of the Sweet Gum trees that covered our little neighborhood. The prickly balls from the trees would crunch under the bare feet of my friends and I as we ran all through the neighborhood. We had a simple life. We played until the sun went down. We climbed trees, we ate the sweet grass that grew next to the ditches, and we put red dirt in frozen pie crust tins and baked the clay in the oven. Everyone in the neighborhood knew everybody else and kids were raised by everybody on the street. If you did something wrong, you got it from whoever caught you. We played with everybody without noticing all of the differences between us. Lil Cliff played with us every summer until his muscular dystrophy got so bad that one summer he showed up in a wheelchair. Poot was always the smelly kid but, we didn't care he was one of us. When we were outside, we were just kids having fun.

Sometimes I would spend time at my grandma's house. She lived in a red and white stripped trailer that sat in the middle of a tobacco field. The house was filled with all kinds of stuff piled up everywhere. The beds in the bedrooms were stuffed into the rooms. They were big enough for multiple people to sleep on and the only other space held a 5-gallon bucket that served as the indoor bathroom and a narrow path to walk out. The rain on the tin roof rocked me to sleep at night and the roosters crowing woke me up at dawn. Every day the routine was get up and dump the bathroom buckets in the field behind the trailer. The big hogs lived in a pen right outside the back door and every morning the pigs had to be slopped. The rickety wooden steps squeaked and swayed as you walked out the door to the pig pen. The grunting and whining of the pigs filled the morning air as they ate the leftovers from the meal from the night before. Collecting the eggs from the old house was a daily adventure. The old house was where my mom and her brothers and sisters lived until it caught fire. Instead of tearing down the burned remains of the house they put a trailer in front of it and the chickens took up residence in the charred remains of the old house. It was

2

like a scavenger hunt to look for the eggs under dilapidated floor boards and inside of old broken furniture. The last chore was walking a mile or so to get water from the well. An old wagon loaded up with buckets was pulled behind us to fill with water. I remember the old well house had an old bicycle tire rim and some frayed rope with a tin bucket tied to the end of it. You would pull the ropes to lower the old rusty bucket down into the well and the bucket echoed as it hit the rock walls going to the bottom where the water was. You could feel the weight of the water as the bucket filled up. Once the bucket was full you'd pull the bucket back up using the old ropes that were wound around the bicycle rim. I can still remember my grandma would always give me the first swig out of the bucket and it was the coldest water that I have ever tasted. We'd make the walk back home with several buckets of water. My grandma would start to cook breakfast at the same time she was making lye soap on an old gas stove. I was always so excited when she would let me light the pilot. I learned in that little country town exactly what is the term running around like a chicken with your head cut off really means. There were always chickens all over the yard. Hens, roosters, and lil biddies that I thought were my pets. My grandma would chase and catch a chicken and once she caught it she would wring its neck. She would swing the whole body around wrapping the neck around her hand and slam it onto the wooden tree stump and cut its head off. The chicken would drop and run around for a few seconds without the head. Once we cleaned off the feathers, she would cut open the chicken and clean it, and that would be breakfast with some chicken broth gravy and biscuits.

The day also consisted of cleaning up, which as an adult seems relative to me. My grandma made brush brooms. She would bundle up long straw needles and tie a piece of twine around the top to hold them all together. My task was to clean up the front yard by using the brush broom to clean up the dirt yard by sweeping away all the chicken shit. Then the rest of the day I would play with the biddies, pick fresh plums off the tree in the front yard, and ride in the old tire swing hanging from the huge oak tree in the front yard. At the end of the day, I would be covered from head to toe in dust. I'd stand by the road waiting for the bus to come and drop off my aunts and uncles. I couldn't wait to see them getting off the bus. My one uncle would always say, "What you been doing all day dirt dauber?" My aunt had a huge dog that would run and almost knock her to the ground when she stepped off the bus. One of my uncles would always run and impress me with his special trick. He could literally run up the side of the oak tree and flip backward and land on his feet.

As simple as that country life was at some point I always made it back home where the torment inside the walls of my home was overwhelming. Seeing my mother beaten almost every day became a part of my life. Seeing her pretend she had lock jaw knowing that my dad had beat her so bad that her jaw was probably fractured. Looking at her take off her robe and seeing the black bruises all over her back as she winced in pain to quickly try to get a shirt on before I could see it. Hearing my mom scream in the middle of the night as she was often beaten at night while I

4

was supposed to be sleeping was not a dream but my reality. My first experience became a constant childhood memory, and I spent a lot of time in my closet crying hoping that things would change.

Chapter 2

I Went Through This

I grew from a very young girl into a young adolescent, spending a lot of time in my closet, hoping and praying that things would change for the better. Things did change…my mom was not the only person being abused. The first time that I was sexually molested by my father I was in a state of confusion and shock. I was not sure what had happened. I was only nine years old. I remember that I had on my favorite outfit that my mom, who was a pretty good seamstress, had made for me to wear on my first day of school. It was a yellow terry cloth shirt with butterfly sleeves and a closure that tied with a bow string in front. I had a green corduroy skirt with pockets on the back and a split that I thought made me cute. I wore a pair of white no-name sneakers. I felt like I was pretty cool that day in my new outfit. My hair was in a ponytail in the middle, and I had one braid all the way around framing my face. That evening I was in my room and my dad came in to talk to me. Sometimes he could be pretty nice; I learned later in life that his being nice was usually always in combination with being high. He told me how nice I looked and that he hoped I had a good day at school. I stood up and twirled around for my dad. As mean as he was, I loved him and wanted to be daddy's little girl. He grabbed me by my waist and picked me up and put me on his lap. He told me that he wanted me to feel how happy he was. I could feel a bump in his pants rising, and I started to squirm to get up. He told me to be still and be quite. He put his hands under my skirt and rubbed his hand on the inside of my thighs. I wasn't old enough to know exactly what was going on, I just knew that it didn't feel right, and I kept squirming trying to get up. He told me to just be quite and let my mom finish cooking. He then pulled my panties over and rubbed between my legs and one of his fingers started going in and out of me as he was moving me up and down on his lap. Then all of a sudden he pushed me onto the floor off of him. I could see a wet spot on his work pants. He said look at what you did to my pants. He told me to stay in my room, and my mom would tell me when it was time to eat. As he walked out he looked at me and said, "This is what daddy is going to do when he wants to show you how pretty you are." He told me I couldn't tell mommy because she wouldn't want to know he thought I was so pretty. This abuse went on for years and escalated into me being held down and penetrated when I needed to be taught a lesson. I hated what he did to me, but I didn't want anyone to know, so I just stayed quiet. I was scared. I was embarrassed.

It almost seemed like I became a target; like I was doing something to have things like this happen to me. I was visiting my uncle and his wife on a Saturday afternoon. My uncle was mowing the grass, and his dog was barking and trying to bite the tires on the lawnmower like he always did. My aunt was working in the plant bed, and I helped her for a while. My cousin was in the house watching TV, and I ran inside because I wanted to watch Soul Train. We watched in the TV room, and we were both dancing and laughing. All of sudden he pushed me down on the sofa and was on top of me holding me down on the chair and trying to kiss me in the mouth and covering my mouth as I tried to scream for my aunt. He held me down with his hand and then pulled his penis out. I was fighting to get up but couldn't. He pushed all of his weight on me. He ejaculated on the floor in front of me. He let me up and told me to get out and stop bothering him. I never asked to go back and visit with my aunt on Saturday's again.

One afternoon it was rainy and cold outside I had ridden the bus home and had the house all to myself. My dad came home and was angry because I hadn't washed the dishes, and I wasn't able to get the fire started in the wood stove. I knew what was coming next because there was no one else home. That day I was not going to allow him to take advantage of me. That day I was tired. That day I knew that what he was doing to me was not right. That day I was willing to die before I was abused again. That day the anger, rage, and hurt that was built up inside me would be unleashed. That day I became the person in power. On that day when my father tried to grab me, I fought back. I picked up a steel poke iron that sat next to the wood stove, and as the tears streamed down my face, I struck him over and over again until his body dropped to the floor. I dropped the poke iron and fell on the floor next to him and I told him, "You will not have me anymore! It's wrong and I won't be quiet anymore." From that day on he never came back in my bedroom, but the abuse did not stop not by a long shot. He abused me in a different way... I was labeled as the girl who had big lips...the girl who's legs were too long...the girl who had a nose that was too big... the girl who would never amount to anything...the girl who would never have a man that would love her... the girl that was a whore just like her mother...the girl who probably wasn't his child anyway...and almost every day from the time I was 14 until I graduated from high school those insults were hurled at me...and those words and violence shaped who I believed I was.

I immersed myself into school because it was the one place that I could find solace. Throughout school I had teachers that impacted me in ways that would shape me as a person. I also had experiences that showed me that I was not the only child going through a bad time at home. I remember going to school with two siblings and they were both very quiet and never caused any problems in class. One day there were people that came to our class to talk to them. The teachers were whispering, and everyone seemed a bit nervous. Around the corner from our class were the restrooms and the two people that were dressed in suits took the brother around the corner away from the other students. I wasn't supposed to, but I snuck around the side to see what was going on. He held his shirt up, and he had these terrible cuts all over his back that were swollen and crusted with blood. As he was speaking, I could see tears streaming down his face. The people took him and his sister out of class that day and I never saw them again. It was rumored that he had been beaten at home with an extension cord and that the state had taken him and his sister away from their mom. I often thought of them and wondered if I told someone of the things that was happening to me at home would the state take me away.

There was one teacher who stood out during my years

in elementary school. She was a graduate of UNC Chapel Hill and was a huge Tar Heel fan! She had an acoustic guitar that she would often play during our class time. I remember the first time I heard her sing, "Puff the magic dragon lived by the sea and frolicked in the autumn mist in a land called Honnah Lee." I was captivated by the sound of the guitar and the beautiful harmonies that were sung. My love of music was born in her class and it transported me from my own existence over the course of my life. Music has always been a comfort to my soul. It always enveloped me and made my darkest times seem not so overwhelming. So, whenever I am asked who my favorite teacher is I always give the same name. Ms. Coates never knew that she played such a vital role in my very survival.

When I went to high school, there was a time that I could have told someone about the abuse that I was enduring at home. One of the principals called me to her office one day just to talk. I'm not sure what I did to trigger her to question me about home, but clearly, she had a sense that something was going on. I walked into her office wearing some high waist button fly jeans, which were all the rage in the late 80's. I sat down in her chair and looked out the window as she talked to me. She asked me what was going on with me and if I needed to talk with someone. I didn't even realize that the stress I was under at home had caused me to lose a massive amount of weight. I was a 5'9" 14- year old freshman girl in a size one jean, and I weighed only about 110 pounds. When she asked, I thought about the twins from elementary school; if I said yes and told her all the horror that existed in my home would the state take me? If I told her that my father sexually abused me for years, would she be able to make it stop? If I told her I had beaten my father to the floor a few weeks before would she understand my pain and help me? I didn't trust her enough, and I covered up the abuse again. If only I had the courage to use my voice and allow her to help me.

Not only was I exposed to abuse, but I was also exposed to the effect that drugs can have on a person. My father was the nicest man in the world; right after he came from outside to smoke his joint. He was funny and had a great personality as long as the Crown Royal was flowing. My parents would throw an all-out party every year for the 4th of July; After all it was my dad's birthday. My mom's whole family would travel for the party. There was always a black pot filled with fish frying and food to feed a full army. There were fireworks and shotguns sounding to cap the July 4th celebration. There was loud music, dancing, and lots of laughter. Everyone was feeling good and growing up I thought that partying, drugs, and alcohol was happiness and it was the way to make life bearable. Little did I know, watching this and equating happiness to this yearly event would one day lead to my own battle with alcohol and drug abuse. I went through all of this and for years after it consumed the person that I was.

Chapter 3

Why Me God?!

In May of 1991, it was almost graduation day. I was excited to be leaving home and heading off to NC A&T State University! I was so looking forward to getting out of the country and moving to the big city of Greensboro. I was getting dressed to hang out with my boyfriend, and for some reason that night my dad was highly irritated with me. As I had gotten older the arguments and fights between us never got better. I was determined that I would stand up to him no matter what. I remember him saying I was too grown and that I needed somebody to show me as I walked by my parents' bedroom into my room. I was listening to music and putting on the finishing touches to head out. As I walked to my closet doors to close them, there was a loud boom and glass came crashing in all around me. My dad had thrown a steel drum that we used to burn trash through my bedroom window. I screamed and threw my arms up to cover myself. I fell to the floor from being hit by the drum. My mom came running into my room and found me laying on the floor covered in glass and soot from the burned trash. My father ran into the room and said that's exactly what I deserved for mouthing off. I was covered in blood there was glass sticking out of my arms and hands. I was screaming at my father how much I hated him and how evil he was. My mom put me in the car, and we headed to the hospital. I remember having the glass dug out of my skin and the doctors talking about possible nerve damage to my arm. I was bandaged up and we headed back home. When we walked in the house, my dad was sitting on the couch watching TV. I immediately picked up the phone and dialed 911. There was no way he was getting away with his cruelty this time. I didn't care who on the outside of our house knew how messed up our family was. My mom called the police and told them I was lying and that I had tried to hurt myself and that 911 assistance wasn't needed. My grandparents came and gave me a talking to. Family didn't call the police on each other. I remember looking at them all and telling them, "Fuck family!"

Only a few people really knew what happened. Everyone else thought I had tried to commit suicide. As long as my best friend and boyfriend knew I was ok. My best friend knew about everything going on in my home. Her mom took me in when I was scared and ran away on several occasions; I spent nights sleeping on their couch. It was easy for me to talk to her she just listened and didn't judge me. She was my confidant, and I admired her. When we were in 8th grade, she survived an insane event in her life. When we were released from school one afternoon there was smoke in the air and the sound of sirens. We were hanging out waiting for band practice to start so, of course, we went outside to see what was going on. When we stepped out on the front entrance, the smoke was billowing from the trees just a few yards from our school. My friend and I immediately took off running up the street. That smoke was coming from her home. When we reached the fire trucks, the fireman stopped us from going any further. My best friend and I stood and watched as the water hoses poured water into her home. Her step- father had set their house on fire, and everything she had was lost. I remember her mother saying we lost material things we didn't lose each other and that is all that mattered. She was one of the strongest people I knew. She also was one of the only people I knew who didn't give a damn about what people thought of her. She would come to school with sweater sets and thigh high stiletto boots and strut around school all day. This girl gave me strength to continue fighting every day.

My boyfriend in high school was a transfer student who moved one neighborhood over from me the summer before our sophomore year. The first time I met him, I was leaving work at the luggage store, and he drove up and stopped next to my car. He looked right at me and said, "I need to know your name right now!" I thought he was a real jackass, but he was so cute. I told him my name, and asked if he was coming to the back to school party. My next door neighbor was having a party that night, and everybody was going to be there. He said I wasn't, but if you're going to be there I will be at the party. I told him that I lived next door and hoped to see him later. I flew home and got myself ready. My dad would not allow me to go to the party, but I could sit on the front porch.

Everybody was parking up and down the road so they had to walk by our house to get to the party. I knew I would see him if I sat on the porch and waited. Sure enough, he and his crew pulled up. He walked right up to my porch and started talking. We were laughing and talking for a while until my dad came out and ran him off. We had managed to exchange phone numbers and the next day I gave him a call. He invited me to come by his house. That afternoon we hung out at his house and threw horseshoes, and it was the most I could remember ever laughing. For the last part of that summer we hung out almost every day. When we went back to school all the girls were trying to find out about the new guy. He was tall and the word was he was on the basketball team. Not only was he on the team, but he was one of the stars of the team. When he asked me to be his girlfriend on 3rd hall in front of his locker I was so nervous. I said yes, and for the next three years we were inseparable. He got to know my family and I got to know his. It was like a fairy tale when I was with him. He was my rock and my protector, but he couldn't save me from the abuse of my father. He knew it was crazy in my house, but he had no clue how bad it was until my arm was injured. He also didn't know that the abuse I endured would lead me to leave him because I didn't know how to be loved.

I had permanent nerve damage in my arm from the glass. School was coming to an end, and it was almost unbearable at home. At least 2 times before graduation my dad had come home and beat me and spit in my face. My mom took a barrage of beatings leading up to my high school graduation. The day after graduation I headed to Greensboro! I couldn't wait to get out of the hell hole that was my childhood home. The crazy part is my mom left too! We packed up all of our things while my father was at work and headed to Greensboro. My mom had gotten a two bedroom apartment for us to live in, and I thought that things would finally get better for us. That move for my mom lasted all of 6 months. At Christmas, my mom decided that living on her own was not manageable and she moved back in with my dad. He had made an "effort" to show how much he had changed. He had joined the choir at church and swore he'd be a better person if she came back home. They got me an apartment off campus and in January I started 2nd semester living on my own off campus.

Living on my own was liberating. Nobody was beating on me at their whim, and I didn't have to find solace in a closet from the fights. I was making new friends that would be with me through the toughest part of my life. They would be the same friends that I would push out of my life when I got to the point that I didn't want anyone that know who I really was around. During freshmen orientation week, we were sitting around waiting for room assignments in Morrison Hall. One of my girls I knew high school and from hanging out in Burlington, NC. We were both chocolate girls and tall, so we naturally gravitated towards one another. Not to mention we were dancing fools! There was one girl sitting in the lobby all by herself. She had a short jet black bob, and she was painting her nails. We couldn't figure out why everybody was scattering away from sitting next to her. So of course we went and sat down right next to her. She was painting her fingernails….black! We looked at each other and almost scattered too until the girl said in a country accent, "Hey, where ya'll from." We both had good ole down home country accents too so, we all began chatting and laughing and at that moment started a friendship that would last a lifetime. I didn't get housing because I decided to stay with my mom, but I hung out with my new girls anyway. In the basement of Morrison Hall, we met a feisty light skinned upperclassman who seemed to know where all the parties were. There was a girl from Baltimore, Maryland that had a thick northern accent and was just as loud as all of us. There was a girl from Reidsville that was ready to party! This was the crew, and we hit campus immediately. We all changed into our cute outfits with the Sam and Libby flats to match in every color. Somebody should have warned us that walking from Morrison Hall to the other side of campus would prove to be a test when the tallest girl in the crew decided to wear a purple skirt, a gold top, and matching gold shoes. I set myself up to be prey for the Omega's, and as soon as they saw my outfit, it was on. The shortest Q on the plot ran across the street and said my boy wants you to be his and you are dressed for the part. He scooped me over his shoulder and delivered me to the middle of the Q plot. My crew stood with their mouths opened as I was abducted. They were then invited to come on the plot too, First day as freshmen and we were hanging out with the most popular Q's on campus.

It didn't take us long to figure out the party girl of the group who had no inhibitions about sex. We were invited to a house party, and of course, the crew was in the house. There was music and dancing and just good ole college fun. There were a few guys there that I knew some of my girls had their eyes on. The party went on for hours, and we played a game called spoons, a version of truth or dare. The spoon would spin and if it landed on you, it was your turn to tell the truth, take a shot, or take on the dare of what was proposed. My choice was always to take a shot, why would I tell these people anything about me, and I certainly wasn't taking a dare. One of our friends always took the dare. She kissed just about every guy in the room, and before the night was over ended up in the bathroom having sex with one of them. This behavior led to a night that has gone down in history as one of the most epic nights on campus.

For anyone that was on campus in the early 1990's you remember or have heard about the infamous Scott Hall train. Our friend, the party girl, had left going across campus by herself. Over the last few weeks, she had been slipping off by herself and spending a lot of time off campus. We could tell something was going on with her. On that night campus was all a buzz about a girl that was held up in Scott Hall having sex with multiple sex partners. We heard about it and headed across campus to see what was going on. Guys were lined up all around Scott. They were laughing and pointing and more and more of them came walking out of Scott joining in on the conversation. One of our homeboys from class saw us all standing around in front of the bookstore and came over and asked where our girl was. We responded with a shoulder shrug, and he busted out laughing. He pointed at Scott and said, "Your girl is a freak! She is in there having sex with any guy that comes in the room." We were stunned. We didn't know what to do we could only stand and hope that she was not the girl everybody was talking about. Over the next few weeks, it became very apparent that she was the girl in Scott and she finally admitted it. We had to cut ties with her simply because you can't hang out with the girl who has sex with almost an entire section of a dorm. She was in a world of trouble, and we didn't want any part of it. Deep down I knew she was coping with something from her past and I knew that she needed a friend, but I was not strong enough to be that person. I allowed her to be degraded and violated. I laughed and snickered about her behind her back and one day sooner than I thought I would be the object of that same ridicule.

There were many other escapades the crew had on campus that fall the most memorable one involved a gun and being pulled over by campus police. While cruising through campus with open containers in the car it dawned on my girl in the back that my brother had left his toy cap gun in the car. She decided it would be funny to pull the gun and shoot at people as we were cruising down the strip. When we got to the end, every other car was allowed to make a left when they passed Cooper Hall. The police flagged us to pull in the parking lot to the right. We were all terrified. I was drinking and driving; there were open containers in the car and.....ole girl had a gun! We knew it was a toy, but the cops didn't. The police stood in the lot facing our car with blue lights flashing and on the bullhorn said, "Get out of the car slowly with your hands up." Before they could even finish the statement, the girl with the gun jumped out spinning the gun around yelling it's just a toy! Only by the grace of God are we all still alive to tell that story.

Every week before the football games we would make our own liquor concoction we called PJ filled with all kinds of fruit and a blend of any liquors we decided to pour in that week. The night before the games were dedicated to doing each other's hair and getting drunk as possible without passing out in the basement. We would drag out on Saturday morning early to get good seats by the band for the game. We would be so drunk by 11:00 am we could barely stand. If a fight broke out in the stands, we would just sit down and let them fight over us because we would be too drunk to move. Our crew gave a new meaning to young and dumb. We were living life and having fun with no regrets. I was enjoying college and the freedom it offered.

My mom seemed to be a bit happier. She would come visit me and hang out. One day when she came to campus, she decided she wanted to get her hair done. The hairstyle that everyone was wearing was finger waves and a rod curl set. We walked from my apartment across campus and went to the Union. Campus and the Union were full of people that day, as it was uncharacteristically warm for an early spring day. The Greeks were out in full regalia, some of the football players were down in the basement at the bowling alley, and my girls were hanging by the bookstore.

My mom and I went to the hair salon in the basement, and we both got our hair done. It was a great day just hanging out with her. I would have never thought that it would be the last day I'd have to just hang out with my mom.

My dad put together a grand gesture of change, and I was impressed. He sang in the men's choir and was talking about trying to become a deacon, but I knew in my heart that he was not changed. He never appreciated church and was mad all the time because my mom wanted to spend so much time in church. As a small child, all the way through high school my mom made sure we stayed in the church and that was the one place my dad was not going on a regular basis. He was what church folks call CEO christens; Christmas and Easter Only. We were involved in every activity that the church had. I was on the usher board and in the choir. We went to Sunday school every Sunday and bible study on Wednesday. My mom was the director of the youth choir, which meant practices and singing at programs all the time. We would go to gospel concerts almost every weekend. The joy that music brought to my life was something that would sustain me over the years. I led songs in church every Sunday when the youth choir sang and when my voice belted out the songs of God I understood exactly what I was singing about. Those songs were implanted into me, and one day the very words that I sang would be the same words that would save my life. The peacemaker act that my dad was putting on lasted until my spring break. I went to DC to visit family and while I was there my father beat my mom pretty bad and tried to stab her with a butcher knife. I guess my mom decided that family does call 911 on family because she filed a police report and took out a restraining order on him. Little did I know that phone call and police report would start the beginning of the end for my mother and life as I knew it.

Now pay close attention because this is where the story pivots. On March 20, 1992, I received a phone call from my neighbor who lived three houses up the road in my hometown and she said, baby, you need to come home. Now you have to remember I am a freshman at A&T, I have an off- campus apartment, its Friday night, and me and my girls were getting ready to hit the town. The Sigma's were having a party, and we were ready to party! When the call came, it started off really strange. She kept saying you need to come home right now... It was really odd to get this phone call from my neighbor and there soon became silence in the room as I was talking to her trying to get her to tell me what was going on. She finally said, "Your mom has been shot and she is being airlifted to Duke Medical Center." The rest of the conversation was a blur. I remember my girls screaming, everybody piling into my car, someone trying to figure out how to drive a stick shift, and heading down 85 South to Durham. I remember there was a full moon and I gazed at it with tears streaming down my face. I was begging God to please let my mom be OK. We pulled up to the ER at Duke and ran inside looking for my mom. A doctor told me to calm down and led me to a room where there were members of my family sitting. My brother was shaking, and his face and eyes were puffy from crying. The doctor came in the room and told us that my mom had not survived. I saw his mouth moving but literally couldn't hear him. All I wanted was to see my mom. I followed the doctor into the hall and begged him to please just let me see her. One of my close friends was holding my hand and stayed by my side the entire time. After much pleading, we were being led into the room where my mom was. They warned me that it was something I didn't need to see, but I had to make sure.

When we walked in the room she was covered by a white sheet. I told them I needed to see her face. I had to make sure it was her. They pulled the sheet from her head, and her head was wrapped in bandages and they were drenched in blood. I felt like my entire body elevated above the room. It was like I was watching all of this from outside my body. My chest tightened, and I couldn't breathe. It was my mom. I grabbed her hand, and for a split second I was elevated with her, and she kissed my forehead and disappeared. I fell to the floor next to the bed. My sweet Dot, my beautiful mother, and her lifeless body lay there on that table and it felt like the weight of the world had been dumped on my body, and I screamed out "WHY ME GOD?!"

I walked back into the room where everyone was sitting, and I felt like they were just gawking at me. They all felt sorry for me, and all I could be was angry. All I wanted to do was get to the monster that had killed my beautiful mother and put a bullet in his head. There was no way he was getting away with murdering my mother. My aunt grabbed me and said calm down baby. Your daddy is gone too. In that moment I learned that my dad had not only murdered my mother, but he had turned the gun on himself too. The phone call that I had with my mother the night before would be the last time I would hear her voice, and the call from my father right after would be the last time I would hear his voice. My father had shot my mother in the head three times and then turned the gun and took his own life. At 19, I was an orphan with a 14- year old brother to take care of.

I was mad, and I wanted to die because God had again allowed me to be this victim of this violence, to hurt in a way that felt like the very breath in my body had been taken away. I grew up in the church. I sang in the choir. I had been baptized in the name of the father, son, and Holy Ghost. I was on the usher board. I knew about God. I knew he was supposed to be a way maker. I knew he wasn't supposed to put more on you than you could bear. Then why had he done this to me? How could there be a God that could be this cruel? I hated him, and I refused to pray to him anymore.

The next week of my life I was numb. I went to my home the next day because I needed to see where my mom was shot. When I arrived, two of my aunts were there and met me at the door. They had cleaning pails and plastic gloves covering their hands. There was blood everywhere. The floor was covered in blood. The sliding glass door that led to the deck were splattered in blood and brain matter. The bar in the kitchen was splattered with blood and pieces of brain particles. I was numb and I couldn't cry. I was angry, and I blamed God for everything that I was going through. I went and lay in my childhood bed and drifted off to sleep and dreamed of my mom; she was happy and laughing and soaring high in the tire swing at my grandma's house. The smile on her face was one of pure joy, and it was so real I could smell her. When I woke up it was still real I wasn't dreaming my mom was dead.

Every step that I made my high school sweetheart was with me. If it hadn't been for him, I don't know how I would have made it through. I headed out to talk with my parents' employers about the burial of both of my parents. My mom's employer was in tears as he told me they would cover all the cost and not to worry about insurance filings or anything that we could figure it all out later. My dad's situation was a bit different. He had committed suicide and his insurance defaulted because he took his own life. I called my dad's parents to talk to them about getting the money together to bury him. I was met by a very abrupt and nasty conversation. I was told that my dad was being buried at the family church and they didn't care where I buried my mom and also that my mom owed them $2500 and they needed their money back. I was stunned. My grandparents were hostile with me after their son killed my mother?! It all stemmed from the fact that I refused to set the wakes or the funeral days for them to be buried together, and I refused to have their burial plots next to each other. My mother was never able to escape him on earth and there was no way I would lay her to rest next to him.

I went to the wake of my mother the next Thursday and her funeral on Friday afternoon. On Friday evening was my father's wake and his funeral was on Saturday afternoon. Those three days almost broke me to the point of taking my own life. My mother was buried in her favorite black wrap dress and her hair was full of curls. The inside of her white casket was lined with beautiful doves ascending into the sky. At the wake my entire body was numb, and I could barely walk on my own. My heart shattered into 1000, pieces and all the tears I had been holding back all came out at one time. I remember long lines of classmates, teachers, and friends hugging me and telling me it would be ok. On the day of her funeral, the walk down the aisle of the church was unbearable. I sat on the front pew looking at her lying in the casket, and all I could think about was when were they going to close the lid. I knew once that lid closed I would never see her face again. When the funeral director came forward and closed the casket to move her to the cemetery, I couldn't catch my breath. All I wanted was for her to wake up. I sat in the cemetery and watched her casket be lowered into the ground beneath the huge oak tree as you walk into the cemetery. I wanted her in that spot so that she would have cover from the tree and be protected from anymore storms.

I didn't attend my father's wake I didn't have the strength to move. I slept in my childhood bed that night and woke up the next morning with a very different feeling than I did when I went to sleep. I woke up mad and pissed off. I went to the funeral home to see my father and he was in a fine suit and one of the most expensive caskets in the building. I told the funeral director that I would not be paying for something that expensive. I then headed to my grandparents' home. When I arrived, I think people could see the vitriol in my eyes and feel the hate that was emitting from my pores. I went straight in and told them that I would not exhaust the small amount of insurance money we were getting on a luxury casket for a murderer and a coward! Being named a beneficiary to my dad's insurance meant the approval for payment of the funeral home came with my signature. I refused to sign the paperwork and demanded he be placed in a cheaper casket, or someone else would need to pay for it. I stood my ground and the change was made. Thinking back on that moment it really didn't matter because the anger I had was not diminished from him being placed in a cheaper casket.

I stayed home for a week after everything was over. My high school sweetheart was right there to comfort me. He truly was a blessing from God in that time of my life. One night as we were going to bed he looked at me and told me that he would always love me and take care of me and that I would never have to worry about being abused again. I looked into his eyes and knew that he meant every word, but I was not able to accept that anyone could love me that way. I hated being in the country where I grew up, and that was exactly where he wanted to be. I was running from my past, and he was happy to live out his life in the place that I was running from.

I went back to Greensboro and attempted to get back to my classes. There was no drive or focus in me, and my advisors knew it. I was directed to withdraw from school and take incompletes for the semester. The only thing I wanted to do was drink and smoke marijuana. I was in a deep state of depression, and my life was spiraling out of control. That summer all I did was drink and smoke myself into a constant state of numbness. That fall when I went to re-enroll in school I found out the advice I was given was not the most informed. I had waited too long to withdraw, and my academic scholarship had been taken away. I was also on one scholarship that was not recurring if you had incompletes from the prior semester. I was on my own to pay my tuition. I took out the max amount of student loans possible for that fall semester, but I was determined to finish college. When we started class, my girls were still right there supporting me. I got a new nickname, Burger. Apparently, I had put on a noticeable amount of weight, and you could see it in my hips and thighs.

Little did I know there was a masterplan being played. In all of my sorrow, hurt, and anger God was still blessing me. All the beer, liquor, and drugs, it did not mean anything to God because he knew what his plan was for my life and the life I would bring into the world. Even though I was mad, I had no faith, I had no hope, and couldn't figure out why me God... God still loved me and would soon show me how his power works even when you have no idea that is what's going on.

Chapter 4

P.J.'s Arrival

God allowed me to wallow in my self-pity for as long as he thought it was necessary. I had been running around drinking and doing drugs like it was going out of style and cursing God every chance I got. I woke up one morning and had my regular start to the day. I drank a 5th of Everclear and skipped my first class so I could watch my soap operas. My girlfriends didn't know I was spiraling the way I was. I had progressed to snorting lines of cocaine, and my grades were in the toilet. In a drunken stupor, I went to economics class. It was too much for me to sit in the class, so I got up and walked out. As I made my way down the stairwell, I lost my footing. When I picked myself up from the floor at the bottom of the flight of stairs that I tumbled down, I realized I had really hurt myself. I made my way to the on campus medical center, but they didn't have X-ray available so they sent me to the public health department to get checked out. When I arrived, they took my vitals and drew blood. The nurse told me that would be back to get me for x-rays. I sat in the office for what seemed like hours until the doctor came in. He asked how I fell down the stairs and I told him it was just a slip on a wet staircase. He looked at me and told me my blood alcohol level was a .15, and I tested positive for marijuana and cocaine. I dropped my head and began to cry uncontrollably. I was so ashamed of what I had become and my heart was so empty that I couldn't stop myself from destroying my life. I knew that I should pray and lean on God and I refused, I hated him and didn't want his help. I told the doctor that I was just having a hard time because my parents had died recently. The doctor said sweetheart you have got to get help and get your life back on track. He looked at me and asked, "Are you at least taking your prenatal vitamins… "Well why would I be doing that," is what I said in my head, "For what"…He looked at me and said you are pregnant! I had no idea! I was running around drinking, smoking weed, and doing cocaine and knew that surely this baby was going to be messed up and I needed to find the nearest place to have an abortion. What the hell did I know about being somebody's mama? I left and went back to campus in a daze. The only thing I knew is that God was just mean and kept asking why me God what did I do to you to make my life so awful. How could I be pregnant? My period was still coming on every month, and I was taking my birth control pills every day. I had to wrap my mind about this development, so I kept it to myself for a while. As I slept that night I dreamed about the last night I talked to my mother and our last conversation. We talked about my new boyfriend and about me being careful and taking care of my body. I was uncomfortable and didn't want to have that conversation with my mom! I woke up that morning very abruptly and heard my mother's voice whisper in my ear softly saying, "Don't forget what I told you." When I sat up in bed, I remembered her last words to me so clearly. She said to me if I ended up pregnant she didn't want to hear anything about me having an abortion! She said I love you and we can get through anything with God! That was God working right then while I was sleeping my mother came to me. I was too dumb to see God's wonder because I was so busy being mad at God. When I woke up that morning I knew two very specific things; I wasn't mad at my mom and I was definitely not mad at my baby and everything I was doing to kill myself I stopped!

At the time I was living in Morrison Hall in the basement and had no idea what I was going to do. It was against the rules to live on campus and be pregnant. I hadn't gained a lot of weight, so I decided I was going to hide the pregnancy for as long as I could. I remember right before we left for Thanksgiving break my dorm director called me into her office. I had put on a few more noticeable pounds and was a bit nervous because she was pretty sharp lady. It wasn't a whole lot that went on in Morrison Hall that she didn't know about. She looked me square in the eye and said, "You know you can't come back here after the break. I will help you find a place if you need me to, but you can't live on campus pregnant." She gave me some contacts to a few apartment complexes and told me it would be ok. I had lost so much in my short time at A&T that this just felt like the end of the world to me.

As I packed up my dorm room, I cried because I was being thrust into this world of adulthood that I was not ready for at all. I had no idea how to care for a baby and no idea how to live on my own, and I also had to tell my estranged boyfriend that I was pregnant and allow him to move on. I knew that the baby was not his. The day he came to my apartment I knew that what I was going to tell him would break his heart. He had held me when I was at my lowest and made me the happiest I had ever been. Over the last four years he had been the most consistent thing in my life, and I was about to break his heart. I just came out and told him I was pregnant and that the baby was not his. The look in his eyes was that of sheer pain. He dropped to his knees and put his hands on my stomach and screamed out, "No! I can be the baby's father. We can still be together. Please don't leave me." We both held each other in tears because I didn't want to let him go. As much as I wanted him to be the father, he wasn't. I lost the love of my life, but I knew it was the right thing to do. I moved into some apartments located just off Church Street. I was still surviving off the money I had received when my parents died; not even realizing that to be sustainable, there needed to be income to continue to live. On Christmas Eve 1992, my entire world as I knew it would change again.

The arrival of my son, Samuel Peterson Hairston, Jr. would be a day that I'd never forget. I went to the hospital on December 23rd around 5 pm. I was in labor all night long. It was the most physical pain that I had ever felt in my life. I was scared because the doctors had warned me about my drinking and drug use and the effect that it may have on my son. I hid the fact that my drinking and drug problem was so bad that it had put the baby in danger from everyone. I was so mad at God that I refused to pray and ask for help. It seemed like every time I asked God for anything it always turned out to be the worst thing that could happen. So, this time I wasn't asking him to make sure my baby was ok because he always seemed to let me down. PJ was born at 7:35 am with the biggest brownest eyes and he was perfectly healthy. The doctor brought him back to me after he was checked over thoroughly and said he is perfectly healthy you need to thank God.

I woke up on Christmas morning and headed home with this little person. For hours we sat on the bed just looking at each other. I couldn't believe that he was mine, and his entire existence was my responsibility. It was the first Christmas without my parents, and his little face spared me the pain of crying for my parents that day. Over the months he grew and picked up on everything quickly. He was a great baby he never cried, and from the day I brought him home he slept through the night. My grandma would fuss at me to wake him during the night to change his pamper and feed him. I told her that I was not using that old school method and interfering with my sleep or his. Every morning he would wake up soggy and hungry, but he was happy and totally rested. Over the course of his 1st year, I was so consumed with learning how to be a mom and watching him grow I didn't have a lot of time to mourn my mother. Although I refused to be thankful to such a cruel God, I know now that he gave my son to me to save my life. My son was my lifeline to make it through the first year of my mother's death. God was still carrying me to meet my destiny to realize my own potential even though the anger I held in my heart made me to blind to see it.

Chapter 5

Love in the Wrong Place

I did my best to be a good mother. I went back to school in January and continued to work towards my degree. I still hadn't figure out that spending money without an income stream would leave me in a dire situation sooner than I thought. I ran out of money from my parents, deaths. I had this little guy looking at me for all of his needs, and I was flat broke. I remember talking to my mom's sister and she told me that I was living in, the real world not a soap opera and I better figure out how to survive. I found myself at the social services building. I applied for food stamps and a monthly check to help me survive. I moved from the nice apartment I was living in to a rough part of the city. I had to drop out of college and lost contact with my girls. My life was based on mourning, struggle, and poverty. There were nights that I fed PJ and didn't eat myself because we had to stretch the food until the next food stamps came. While struggling I started drinking and using drugs again. And from that point, I started hanging with people who were much different than the people I had known in my life. This guy was hanging out at my apartment with some girls one night while we were smoking weed and said you need to use what you got to get your money right. He told me men would pay to see me with my clothes off because I was a beautiful girl. He was a DJ in the local strip club and said he could get me an audition if I wanted to make some real money.

My friends and I decided that we were due some

hangout time since I had been out of the loop for so long. My grandparents took PJ for the weekend, and we set out on an epic adventure to Atlanta, Georgia to experience Freaknik. Freaknik was an annual event attended by the majority of Historically Black College and University students. This celebration included candy coated old school cars, street festivals, concerts, and a ton of drinking and smoking weed. Me and my girls hadn't seen a party we didn't want to be a part of so we decided we were heading to the party in Atlanta. We piled up five deep in a Suzuki Sidekick and hit 85 South to the A to party for two days! When we got there on Friday night, the city was packed. There were cars and people everywhere. Music was booming from car stereos, and girls had apparently lost all inhibitions at Freaknik. There were girls completely naked dancing on top of cars. The atmosphere was something that we had never experienced before. When we finally made it to our hotel, we got dressed and hit the town. It was much easier to walk than it was to drive. We were scantily clad with the shortest daisy dukes we could find. And our shirts stopped mid drift because you couldn't be out if you weren't showing off your abs with the Janet Jackson belly chain. Everything about that night was built around walking, going in and out of different parties, and drinking as much free liquor as possible. When we got back to the hotel the sun was coming up. We slept for a while and got up to go back out in Atlanta. There was a free concert in Piedmont Park and the sheer mention of Outkast in the 90's and it was the place to be. There were thousands of people spread out across the park for as far as the eyes could see.

The music was loud, and the party was jumping. There was a sense of freedom and unity in the park until it happened. The gunfire was in the distance, but when the gun sounded the sea of people that were dancing and rapping along became a swirling wave of panicked party- goers. As we stood close to the stage you could see the people running in our direction like a massive tsunami knocking down everything in its path. We started running as fast as we could not to get trampled. We had been separated and had to figure out how not to be crushed. I grabbed to a power pole that was in my path and wrapped myself around it and held on as tight as I could. The crowd of thousands avoided the pole and holding on to it I'm sure saved my life. After the commotion died down it was time to try and find my crew. It wasn't like I had the luxury of pulling out my iPhone and calling we still had pagers and needed a payphone to make a call. Cell phones were big ticket devices back then, and not everyone had them. I started to walk back in the direction of the hotel and hoped that everyone would head back in that direction too. On my way to the hotel I was stopped by a group of guys and knew that I needed to get away from them as quickly as possible. There was another girl that didn't get across the street fast enough, and as I cut through traffic, I looked back and saw that they had picked her up off the ground and several of them had their hands under her dress. She was screaming for me to help her, but I kept going. I was scared and didn't want to be assaulted again. I had lived through that so many times in my life that I was too weak to help her. Again assault had found its way into my life; I had allowed someone to be victimized and didn't try to help them. That time in Atlanta I saw women doing all sorts of crazy things that made men throw money at them. When I got back to Greensboro, I started thinking about how to get me some extra cash and get out of struggle mode.

A few weeks later I was strapped for cash. I owed the girl I was living with money for my part of the rent, and I had no money for food. I picked up the phone and called my DJ friend. He told me to come in the next night. Me and my roommate went out and picked me an electric blue, sequin, two piece set and some black booties. I had no money so we were out shoplifting to get these items. She had some old weave left in her hair bag so she glued it in and she cut it into a shoulder length bob with Chinese bangs. She helped me practice some moves for my first night as a stripper. When I arrived at the club, I immediately noticed my outfit was not like the other girls and the heels on my shoes were nowhere near high enough. My dance moves were nothing in comparison to what I saw on the stage. Girls were doing splits and flips and hanging from the pole in the middle of the stage. By the time it was my turn I was terrified, but I needed the money, so I walked out on stage when I heard the name I had been given called. On that night Entice was born. I did my terrible moves and walked and crawled around on that stage for what seemed like an eternity. The DJ talked to me afterward as I counted the money that had been thrown on the stage. As I counted, I was amazed at how quickly I had made over $100. He looked at me and said you need to take that money and get your game up you can make some real money and said next time make sure you remember to take your top off. I spent the next week going to different clubs just observing the girls. I got a few new outfits and some 6- inch heels. I found a new club to work in, and Entice evolved into a known name in the clubs and it was common knowledge on campus what I was doing. It was ironic I was the object of ridicule for my choices and one night saw the girl from Scott Hall. She was dancing in the same club as me, and at that moment I felt ashamed and dirty. I had fallen to the likes of my one time friend dancing in the club for money. I then realized that I was no better than anyone else in that club. I made some new girlfriends that were there to make money just like I was. I stopped hanging with my college friends and lost full contact with them. My new friends were like me we all in some way were broken. We were together almost every night, so we became close and we took our show on the road. Every weekend my grandparents were watching my son for me, and I went to work.

We danced up and down the east coast from NY to Atlanta. We could make enough money in one weekend to take care of our expenses for a whole month. That ugly girl that was too tall and legs were too long was a feature act and was able to take care of her son. For a few years, I lived the life of a stripper. I stayed up all night and got high. I played with men's emotions to have them give me money and pay my bills. There was one guy that caught the worse of Entice, but he probably deserved it. We dated for a few months, and he paid bills and provided free drugs to our apartment. He drove us to several out of town feature shows. The one thing he did wrong was leaving his flip phone open and getting caught by his wife! She contacted me to let me know I was dating her husband. She had been suffering from a serious medical condition that required brain surgery, and she couldn't believe that he would do this to her. My response was laughter as I told, her, "I am not married to you, so you need to check your husband not me." The next time he came over to the apartment he was met with a cast iron frying pan to the face and dragged into the apartment. We took all of the money out of his pockets, took all his jewelry, stripped him down to his underwear and rolled him back outside the door. A note was stuck to him saying, "Stay your married ass at home with your wife!"

I spent hours talking to club patrons about how fake and judgmental people were. I talked about why I was there, and my purpose for being in the club was not because I had this overwhelming desire to be a stripper, but because my main goal was to take care of my son. I had the typical stripper line; I was there to get on my feet and pay my way through college. No matter how strong and tough I appeared on the outside, on the inside, I was ashamed of what I was doing. I was broken and had a false sense of who I was. I was still running from the demons of sexual abuse. I had no direction and no purpose. I was still mad at God, and I refused to live by what his purpose was for my life. I refused to pray and I refused to forgive him for ruining my life. During my time in the club I made a few friends that seemed to be a lot like me. We hung out and we talked about how we ended up in the club. Some of the stories from the women were horrific. Even though we were all struggling, God had a way of putting together the girls that needed each other the most. We had cookouts on the weekend, and a few of the girls became very close to my son. He had some strong women around him, even though we still had a lot of work to do we all loved him and tried to instill the best in him. Some of those friendships would blossom into a lifetime of friendship and support.

After a few years, I was tired and wanted to do something different with my life. I had met a man that had some money, free drugs, came from a good family and wanted to marry me, so I went for it. I was tired of struggling and dancing, so I got married. It was during those years that I relieved the abuse of my childhood but in a different capacity. I was maturing as a woman and a mom. My baby was playing youth sports, and I wanted to be a better mother for him. I loved my little boy unconditionally, but my personal life was still a mess because I was still broken.

Maintaining in a marriage that was based on a lie was torment. There were many nights that I was home with my kids and my husband never came home. Everyone in the town knew he was in the street with other women and I'm sure looked at me wondering why I stayed. I asked myself that question every day. I remember standing in a mirror one day at my lowest point. The kids and I were home after a long day of fundraising for one of the kid's youth basketball teams. I had donated food and my husband never came home to bring the products the morning of the fundraiser. I scrambled around trying to find what I could so nobody would know he didn't come home. The entire day I was agitated and conflicted. As I stood in that mirror, I decided that the best thing I could do for everyone was not to be around. I unwrapped a straight razor that I found in my medicine cabinet in the bathroom. As tears streamed down my face, I laid the point of the razor on my left wrist. I replayed in my mind some of the awful things I had seen my mother endure and thought if I were dead I could finally be with her. I pressed the razor into my skin and saw the blood, and as I began to pull the razor to slit my wrist, there was a loud knock on the door. BOOM! BOOM! BOOM! My middle son yelled out, "Mama, mama come quick we need you!" I dropped the razor in the sink as my wrist was dripping with blood. As I looked at myself in that mirror I heard a very faint voice say to me, "You are not this, and this is not what you were put here to be." I was terrified and rambled through the drawers and cabinets to find some Band-Aids so I could clean myself up. I rushed out to see what my kids needed, but that was a defining moment in my life. What was that voice and why was it talking to me?

When I finally got my husband on the phone he had been missing for a full 24 hours. This wasn't the first time or the longest amount of time he had been missing. Instead of apologizing, "He told me he wished I would find somebody else to talk to so I would stop asking him so many damn questions." As I stood back in that same mirror, I realized I had let myself go. I was at 245lbs and a size 22. My lips were too big, and my legs were too long. I was that same ugly little girl that would never amount to anything and would never have a man that would love me. I was determined that I would get myself together and show him exactly what he was going to be losing. Little did I know I needed to get myself together from a childhood of abuse that clouded and misguided everything in my adult life. I had married my father and was living the life of my mother.

The next summer I was back in shape and in a size 10 and I looked hot! Instead of praying and allowing God to order the steps in my life to address a bad marriage gone to worse I did it my way. I started smoking weed again, and I hit the club ready to mingle and find me somebody that would occupy my time just as my husband had found several people to occupy his. I stepped out in some skin tight tan linen shorts that barely covered my butt cheeks. My shirt was a black, tan, and cream animal print, backless halter top with a low cut front. My shoe game was so fierce as I strutted in 4" wedges made of mohair in zebra print. The wooden bottoms clicked with every stride I took. I knew exactly how to attract men from my days in the club. That night me and my girls had drinks backed up at the bar. The waitress was waiting on us to finish drinks to clear our table to bring out more. As we laughed, danced, and controlled the eyes of every man in the club one man decided that he was brave enough to take the chance after seeing several others dismissed from our area. He walked up looking like a Greek God. His shoulders were broad; his skin was sun kissed and dark as coal. His teeth sparkled as he asked me to dance. When I stood up, he looked down at me and said with a thick accent from the motherland that this would be the dance that made me his queen. I was drawn to him like a moth to a flame. We danced and laughed for what seemed like hours. When I finally got back to our section, he asked if he could use my phone to call his brother who he was riding with. I handed him my phone, and while he held the phone to his right ear, he took a phone out of his pocket and received the call he was making. He looked at me and said now I have your number in my phone and you have mine.

That summer my intention was to inflict as much pain on my husband as he had inflicted on me; living through years of infidelity with random women. I dated this man in plain sight of everyone. We went bowling; we played pool at the local billiards joint, and we kissed passionately for the entire town to see. The reckless abandon I showed was tiring. I spent the night with this man and traveled with him on out of town trips. And while it was embarrassing to my husband it was more embarrassing to me. I allowed myself to be lowered to a standard that I detested. In the effort to hurt someone the way they had hurt me and exact my own revenge I degraded myself. After months of this behavior, I stopped and made a plan to make some real changes in my life. This is not the person that I wanted to be and definitely not the person that I wanted raising my children. The days of Entice and living from party to party were over, and I didn't want that life again. I was through with looking for love in all the wrong places it was time for me to love myself.

Chapter 6

The Time Has Come

The time in my life had come for me to get my act together. I knew that the voice that I heard in that mirror was God and he began to work on me. Not only was I tired of being angry with God he was done allowing me to be. The first thing I did was find a counselor. For as much as I had gone through I had never enlisted the help of a professional to guide me through my mourning and anger. As I sat talking to my counselor, the first visit I broke down and cried most of the session. I was that little country girl again, scared and sobbing in the closet, and for months she worked with me to retrace the steps of my childhood and my adult life to that point. I remember her saying to me one day I am truly amazed that it took this long for you to get help and more amazed that you didn't hurt yourself or someone else living with all the pain, anger and grief. In fact, I had hurt myself by tarnishing my reputation. I had hurt my children by becoming someone that was not fit to be a mother gallivanting in the street like a single person again. Knowing that one day, I would have to look them in the face and tell them about my past. The only thing I could say was that it must have been God all along. And at that moment I realized that no matter how mad I was at God he was always by my side making sure that each step was one of purpose for what he had planned for my life.

I walked into the church on Sunday morning for the first time in years. The serenity that rushed over my body was a feeling that calmed my soul and lightened my footsteps. I listened to the word and songs as they filled the air. I was loyal in attending church every Sunday even if I couldn't get anybody else in my house to wake up and go. I knew that I had to be there. I remember the choir singing, "Can't nobody do me like Jesus he's my friend." It took me back to my home church in Caswell County where I grew up singing in the choir and leading songs. When the announcements came in church that day, it was a call for anyone wanting to become a member of the gospel choir or sing on the praise and worship team. That following Monday I showed up for both rehearsals. I was informed that I would need to become a full member of the church to join the choir. The next Sunday I was led by God to the alter, and I recommitted my life to Christ. I screamed out the name of God and the release from my body caused me almost to pass out. I had finally broken the chains that had me bound for so long. The hopelessness and despair that had hung around my neck like an albatross had been lifted and thrown away. I went through new member classes and one month later I was baptized again in the name of the father the son and the Holy Ghost, and my anger and hatred of God was washed away. As I was dipped down into the water visions of my childhood flashed before me. I remembered being dipped in the water outside in a pool by the church. It was cold, and I was scared and really didn't know why. This time I knew why I was being dipped and as the choir sung, "Take me to the water to be baptized," tears rolled down my face. The God that I had fought so hard to hate for many years had accepted me back as his child. My slate was washed clean, and he still loved me in spite of all my wicked ways. I sang in the choir and used my voice just as my grandma had always fussed at me about doing. I sang praises to God and he talked to me and the more I praised him, the easier life seemed to be. I remember talking with my pastor one day and he said you are still a baby in Christ. I know that there is a special anointing in you. If you continue to follow his steps the voice that you continue to hear will become louder and louder and before long it will drown out all the doubt that the devil will try to place in your heart. He told me that I was destined to do great works and to always remember to lean on God. It was not always easy to stay on the right path and just like anyone else I stumbled along the way, but the falls made me stronger because I knew where to look for my strength to continue to fight.

The next step was to enroll myself back into college. I was an honor student and not having a college degree was not an option. My calling in life was not to work at drive-thru windows and pack fast food bags. Not that it's anything wrong with that work, but I knew that it was not for me. I went back on the campus of A&T for the first time since I had dropped out. It all seemed surreal as if it had been a lifetime since I had been on campus for anything. I went and got copies of my transcript in order to complete my application for Guilford College. I was determined to get my life back on track and get out of the situation that had me bound by the financial inability to survive on my own. I swore that once I dug my way out I would never allow myself to be financially dependent on another man. Guilford College was a life changer for me.

The spirit of activism and social justice that runs through the very fabric of the institution transformed me. Learning about everything from the great tribes of Africa to the Harlem Renaissance I was catapulted into a world of knowledge that I had forgotten I had a thirst for. Guilford College quenched my thirst and gave me new directions in so many areas of my life. I re-engaged my love for music and took acoustic guitar lessons. I sang songs and played my instrument with the passion that I had as a child. I worked on social justice issues that impacted my community. I became a trained community organizer looking to make a difference in the world. I taught classes and read books. I was finding myself again in ways that I had let be buried by sorrow and anger. My years at Guilford College taught me about loving myself and loving the things and people that I allowed to be in my life. The last thing I had to do was become financially independent, and with a little luck, I broke into the world of corporate America. The peace that I had found in giving up my anger and hatred freed me on a level of unbelievable joy. I did my time, and I had come to take back my life.

Right after my college graduation I moved into my own apartment, and for the first time in my life I was clear on what I needed to do to be a responsible adult. I worked hard and paid my bills. I focused all of my attention on my kids and work and making a good life for us. In that process, God's blessings continued to rain down on my boys and me. I moved through getting a promotion on my job every year. My oldest son became one of the top basketball recruits in the country, and with that blessing on his life God was setting me up for one of the biggest challenges I would ever face in my life. The time had come for my true faith in God to be tested to its core.

Chapter 7

The Carolina Way

My oldest son was one of the most talked about basketball players in America during his high school career. The recruiting process was something that you couldn't plan for. You barely see it coming, and when you find out, everybody else seems to know already. I knew he was a good basketball player from middle school basketball and competing on the AAU circuit for years. I hoped that he would be lucky enough to attend college for free one day on a basketball scholarship. There was something else that also became clear. People did not care about my child or his feelings, and that was very evident during one of his middle school games. One of the hardest things that I ever had to do was sitting my son down and telling him some things about my past. At one of his games, one of the dads of another player walked up on me and said, "What's up Entice you still looking good." I was mortified and embarrassed beyond belief, and I knew that I had to tell my son before anyone else told him. I explained to him that a few years before when he and I were struggling and sometimes didn't have food to eat or the lights would be off that I decided to do something to make us some money. I told him that I was an exotic dancer for a few years and some people recognized me and I wanted to tell him and explain before somebody tried to embarrass him. His reaction as a 13- year -old boy was priceless. He looked at me and said, "You was as stripper?!" There was a long pause as he processed this information and I looked at him wondering why my 13- year- old knew what a stripper was. He then looked at me and said, "Mama I love you no matter what you have done. You're my mama and one day I'm gonna take care of you."

In 9th grade basketball, all started coming together but, I did have a struggle on the academic side. He was now a strapping 6'3" physical specimen. He was still ADHD, and that combination made it difficult for some teachers to deal with him. He was still delayed in turning work in on time, but got the job done with some extra tutoring. There was one particular teacher that called me in for a conference to talk about his performance. We sat in the principal's office and discussed his lack of concentration and the fact that in her words he had a "menacing" appearance. Now mind you the school had a standard mode of dress policy, so he looked no different from any other child in his khakis and blue collared shirt. So my question was if the conference was about his performance and how to keep him on track what did his appearance have to do with anything. She responded by saying she felt uncomfortable helping him after school alone because of his size and she wasn't sure if his ADHD made him aggressive or not. I let her have a piece of my mind that day. My son was profiled based on his size. A student that has an IEP and needs extra help should be able to get it. It was not his fault this teacher was 5' tall and intimidated by a large black male. I told her to keep her stereotypical rhetoric to herself and had him moved to another class. What was really baffling was that after he became a star basketball player this same teacher approached me and told me what a fine young man he was.

My response to her was, "He was a fine young man when you didn't know he played basketball too." I never knew that the feelings of outrage I had about him being objectified because he was larger in stature and black would follow him many different places in life.

My son was trying out to play varsity basketball at one of the most successful and notable high school basketball programs in North Carolina. When he made the varsity team, it was pretty exciting and when the season began being a freshman starter at this school was unheard of. I had my first experience with notoriety on a local media level because he was attending a school that some felt was outside of our residential area. I had moved and was going through a divorce and it was really nobody's business where we lived, where my kid was going to school, or what paperwork I turned in to make sure it was all on the up and up. So, I said nothing and ignored all the gossip. He had a really great season and that summer is when it all blew up. He attended Nike All- American Camp in St. Louis, and after that, the mail started rolling in and the calls started coming.

That next season is when I finally realized what everyone else seemed to already know. My son was a high major DI basketball recruit and the people I would meet, and places I would go because of it were unbelievable. One of the first games of the season Roy Williams was at his game, and as a lifetime Carolina fan I was so excited and asked who Roy was there to see. The man in the stands looked at me, with a bit of confusion, and said, "He's here to see your son." I learned very quickly that he would not be the only big time coach I would meet. Over the next year, coaches from every major college and university in the country were recruiting my son. We visited different campuses and attended games in several arenas. News articles were being written about him and about how great he was as a player. He was recognizable by basketball fans everywhere we went. We attended UNC basketball games the entire season of the 2009 championship season, meeting former players and coaches on every visit. People that I grew up admiring were all vying for my son to be a Tar Heel. Phil Ford was talking to him at one game and said, "I heard you would like to wear your high school number in Chapel Hill. If it takes letting you wear #12 to get you here, I can make that happen." Phil Ford a UNC icon wanted my son in Carolina Blue. The first time I ran into Dean Smith in the halls of the Dean Dome I was in tears. My childhood idol my favorite coach of all times it was so surreal that my son could be a part of this legacy. The summer after his sophomore year he was scheduled to attend an elite camp at Duke University, and I assumed that a possible offer would be made during that visit. UNC came in and made an offer just days before the camp, and the rest is history. The day after Roy Williams called our home on his way home from the beach and made a scholarship offer PJ committed to play basketball at UNC!

For another year he competed at his local high school, but the newspaper clippings and UNC notoriety was not only too much for him to handle it was too much for the adults preparing him for college to handle. He was being given too many opportunities to be irresponsible without

52

consequence and I knew it was because he was a "star". He had put on a massive amount of weight, and his work ethic was noticeably lower. He was buying into his own hype and I wasn't having it! I talked to his teachers and told them he needed to be made to turn his assignments in on time just like everyone else. How would he be prepared for a college syllabus being allowed to just float by? I went to the coaches and told them he needed to get his weight down. He was going to UNC to play shooting guard, not Defensive End. Nobody took me seriously, and it was frustrating. I know that it was not intentional, but I was just a mom who really didn't understand the recruiting process to them. The straw that broke the camel's back was one evening when my teenage son decided my rules of not being able to leave going out with friends at 1 am were too strict for him to follow and ran away from home. I sat on my couch and didn't move a muscle. I refused to chase after an angry child who was clearly losing their way. My job was to figure out how to get him back on the right path. He ended up at a teammate's home and spent the night there. His teammate's parents didn't even call to let me know he was there and ok. I'm sure they were just letting him cool off, but I never understood how you could not tell another parent knowing that they were possibly out looking for him and surely worried. As a mom who is known to take no junk, that one outburst was all it took for me to make some drastic changes for the next school year. I got on the phone and called around to several highly influential prep schools. One coach told me he wouldn't consider him because he was asked by his friend not to go after this particular player. I respected the loyalty and moved on. I finally found a program and a coach that I believed would be a good fit. His senior year was spent in a military uniform sleeping in a cinderblock room on a twin- sized bunk bed. Hargrave Military Academy would deal with the fame and all that came with it. The military lifestyle did wonders for his personality and his grades! For many years school was a struggle not a failing effort but a struggle. Being ADHD offers challenges that you can only understand as a parent who has raised a child with ADHD.ADHD meant having teachers not understand why your child would get up and just walk around class during instruction time. ADHD meant having counselors on one side telling you that your child should be heavily medicated if he didn't want to end up in special needs classes. ADHD meant having family members question why you can't handle your child and their bad behavior. ADHD meant family members criticizing you for choosing to use medication management to help your child succeed. ADHD meant often times questioning if all the drugs and alcohol you consumed had damaged your child. For many years the struggle with the disease affected every aspect of school for my son. When I chose to send him to Hargrave, it was the first time I felt confident that my son would be in a situation to thrive academically and be given the tools to be equipped to handle the rigors of being a college athlete.

The spring was a great time of year for him. He had put in the work and had been selected to compete in the McDonalds All- American Game in Chicago, Ill. It was the trip of a lifetime. Me and a bunch of friends and family all piled into a black SUV and made the almost 12 hour drive to cheer him on. It was cold and windy, but the electricity in the windy city air was magical. Watching my two younger sons experience this was amazing. They were in awe of the huge buildings, but more in awe of the basketball players they were meeting. Every star player they had seen on TV was in the hotel. I remember my middle son saying my brother is a star too he was so proud! The atmosphere in the dunk contest and 3pt contest was breathtaking. We knew he would be in the 3pt contest because he was one of the best shooters in the country. We got a huge surprise when he was placed in the dunk contest too because one of his fellow All American's had gotten hurt and couldn't participate. He did an awesome job and was in 1st place after the 1st round. He didn't win either contest, but he was there and created memories that would last a lifetime. We attended the game the next evening and the Chicago Bulls arena was packed. People from all over the country came to watch these high school kids play basketball. The experience was one that changed the way I looked at the process of going from high school to college as a star athlete. The things that you are blessed with no matter how unreal they seem were ordered by God and it was an amazing feeling of blessings and lessons along the way.

Immediately after graduating from high school, he was off to UNC for his first session of summer school and he was doing great. He was having the time of his life. All I could think about were my parents, who were both huge UNC fans, not being here to experience this dream. But we had family and friends who had watched him grow up around us to help cheer him on and everyone was super excited. I was anxiously waiting on the day that he would run out of the tunnel with fans cheering in the Dean Dome and the pep band playing the fight song. The first night was at Late Night with Roy, an event we had attended several times before, but this night it was my son being announced. As the crowd cheered and screamed, tears streamed down my face as his name was announced and the roar of the crowd rose into the rafters. All I could do was thank God for such an amazing blessing. I had done what I didn't even believe I could do myself. I had lived through the darkest of times in my life and on that night my cup was overflowing with blessings. As the season progressed it was crazy, he got some playing time and was playing well. He made the All-Tournament team at the Las Vegas Invitational. I attended an inaugural event of epic proportions. I boarded an aircraft carrier called the U.S.S. Carl Vinson to see my son play in his camouflage uniform. President Barack Obama and First Lady Michelle Obama sat in front of me courtside. When my son made a 3pt shot the President said, "Nice shot PJ." It was the best cheer ever! It seemed like it was going to be a great year. Unfortunately, as we moved closer to conference play, his playing time decreased, and shooting percentage struggled. His freshman year ended up not being one for the record books for sure. As he struggled, the world of social media that was once his biggest cheerleader became dogged in its analysis of him. He kept working and getting ready for his sophomore year. And I kept telling myself that the media and fans were just background noise.

Sophomore year got off to a great start. He was playing well and shooting the ball well, and I knew he would shine in that year's campaign. We spent Thanksgiving in Hawaii for the Maui Invitational. It was still hard for me to grasp that I had gone from a lil country girl covered in dust to being the mom of a college basketball star. The time in Hawaii was magical, and a half court buzzer beater was a great part of the excitement. There was a huge push by fans and media attention directed on why he wasn't starting. I, of course, wanted him to start as any mother would, but I also respected coach, and knew he could do his job much better than I could. So again, I had to block out the fans and media and trust the coach that I allowed to coach my son to do his job. Before the season ended my son was a starter for UNC! There were so many exciting moments and scary moments during that season. I attended one game in Boston, and he was kicked in the head, and he was knocked out and laying on the court in Boston College. Being texted by literally 100's of people saying they saw me on the court on ESPN and that they had no clue I was his mom. It was terrifying being in a city as a single mom and not knowing if he would be ok. That year at the ACC tournament he was playing great, and in the game against Florida State, the ball was stripped from his hand. I was yelling at him to take care of the ball when I saw him hold his hand up and it was gushing blood. I watched the trainers work on his hand from the stand and when they wrapped his hand and immediately took him off the bench to the back of the coliseum and once again, I was back on camera as I left my seat and jumped over the railing to the floor of the coliseum to find out what was going on with him. In the back of the coliseum, he laid on a table as the doctors sterilized the area and prepared him for stitches. The doctor said, "Well at least there is no ligament damage." I asked him, "How do you know that?" He held PJ's hand up and said, "Look!" As I looked inside the inside of his hand my stomach got weak, but I didn't waiver, I grabbed his hand because I knew the sight of blood made him panic and said, "Suck it up kid the doctor is going to have you all fixed up in a few minutes." The webbing between his middle and index finger was completely ripped open, and I knew his ACC Tournament was over. To mine and everyone's surprise he came out and played the next night with a concoction on his hand that looked like an oven mitt! He played bandaged up through the NCAA tournament.

The season was a whirlwind of games and travel, and it was all worth it! At the end of the season he was the leading scorer and most improved player and we celebrated him and the entire team at a sports banquet that always felt like a huge family dinner. With the end of the season came the next step in preparing for junior year and that was the never ending question of, "Will you come back for your junior year or will you leave for the NBA." It was crazy because nobody knew our intentions about college, but a successful season sets the media into a frenzy to figure out the answer and scoop the next outlet. Our intention was always to stay at UNC for four years and graduate in a sea of Carolina Blue in Kenan Memorial Stadium. When the decision was made, an announced that he would be returning for his junior year I never in a million years imagined that the summer of 2013 would change the way I felt about UNC and my son.

In the early hours of June 6th I received a telephone call that said your son had been arrested! I felt my heart crumble in my chest. Before I even knew any details I went into protect mode and instantly thought, what can I do to help my child. That is what a parent does. That is what unconditional love allows you to do. The details of the arrest are now coming over the phone. My child had not listened to the advice of his mother. I recognized some of his friends were not part of the UNC family. He was driving without a license after I implored him to get his license before going back to school his sophomore year. I had even fixed up my old 740 BMW to give to him, but he didn't listen. There was marijuana found in the car, not on any person in the car, but in the car under a floor mat in the third row of seats. The minimal amount found was grounds to take him along with 2 of his buddies into the Durham County police station to be charged with possession of less than a ½ ounce of marijuana and driving without a license. The media flurry exploded the next day. His name was on the ESPN ticker for what seemed liked months. And the same media I had worked so hard to ignore refused to be ignored. The same fans that had loved him vilified him.

Journalists revealed that a hit on their Twitter was far more important than an accurate account of what happened. The sensationalized stories could not be combatted. One news outlet ran the police report, and the incident report, simultaneously as if it were one document. At that point, in the media, he went from having a small amount of marijuana to having a felony amount and a loaded gun. The police investigation notes were leaked to the press. The media did not print the actual document, but printed excerpts to play into the sensationalized narrative they were creating.

The next thing that happens is an outcry from a rival fan base with an ax to grind with their neighboring nemesis. The rental car is called into question. Who rented the car was it the reported "agent". The "agent" was a native of our home town and attended the same high school as my son. Our family had known him for years and at no time was he a registered sports agent. He worked with special needs children and mentored young athletes in our community. He was a friend of our family. The media had no clue that the NCAA did not come to UNC to investigate about rental cars and the traffic incident. The NCAA was scheduled to speak to me on June 6, 2013 to discuss our relationship with our family friend. We knew he had moved and was working to become a sports agent and reported that as soon as we knew and also cut communications with him at that point. One thing I knew was the rules and did everything to abide by them.

Before I go into detail about my experience with the NCAA, there are some things that you need to understand about dealing with the NCAA and how it works. Because they come in just to ask questions, there is not a formal investigation initiated. The questioning phase is just to gather information because an allegation had been made. Keep in mind that because this is not a formal investigation you are not allowed to know what they are looking for. You are not given the information about who made the allegations or what information they have collected. At the point that the NCAA questions you it has been taken as fact what has been alleged is true, and it is now your job to prove your innocence, but to prove it without having the ability to know or even cross- examine your accuser. In my world, that means you are guilty until proven innocent, which is not how our country or legal system works. However, in the nonprofit world of the NCAA, there is a different set of rules. The *Kafkaesque nature of an NCAA investigation is brutal.* Also, there are rules of jurisdiction outlined in their own bylaws that are clearly not followed. An athlete is bound to give them all information that they have access to when asked. As a parent, you are not bound by any NCAA jurisdiction and have no responsibility to hand over any information that they request if you choose not to. However, be mindful that if you don't cooperate, they will then punish your child, which to me is very similar to the way the mafia was run. You can choose not to cooperate, but in turn, know that I will burn your house down. This is some real power that is wielded by a nonprofit organization!

So back to the way the questioning was handled from the beginning and how it snowballed into a seven month journey with this nonprofit group. I will also intertwine in this account how the media's role was played out as well. The first NCAA interviews took place on June 20, 2013. I would like to note that on June 21, 2013, a full report was posted online that had specific information about this interview that only people in the room would have privy to. So for me, the level of security and confidentiality that I was guaranteed was breached from the very beginning. I was asked for my bank records, receipts for all of my away game travel expenses (specifically Hawaii), and my telephone call logs/text logs. My son was asked for all of his bank records, telephone call/text logs. There was a deadline placed on this request, and all of the information would need to be turned over. All of our bank records, receipts and credit card statements were submitted and clearly showed that a wire transfer in the extremely large sum they were looking for was a ludicrous accusation. However, there were a few obstacles that were in the way of getting some information requested turned over. Let's talk now specifically about what was not turned over. My phone records belonged to my employer and due to the sensitive nature of my job and possible negative ramifications it could cause the company if information was leaked, which was appearing to be a running theme with this questioning as blog spots were jumping with inside information as well. Keep in mind I was under no jurisdiction to turn the records over, but was willing to do so voluntarily if my employer had allowed it. The NCAA contacted my employer to work out a "deal" to get the records. When my employer told them to send in writing what they would like, they were never heard from again. I can only assume they didn't submit an additional request for the records in writing because they had already been told no, had no rights even to ask my employer per their own bylaws, and no subpoena power which meant access denied. Phone records were requested from June 2012-June 2013. His phone was not in his name until December 2012 and the person that owned the phone line from June 2012-Dember 2012 was not willing to get involved and was not required to do so. Phone logs that we had access to, December 2012-June 2013, were submitted. The text logs were another issue. Only 90 days of text logs are available from cell phone carriers, and we were asked for 12 months of logs. There was a delay in deciphering which dates were requested, and in that time frame our attorney went on vacation. Because of the delay, caused by the NCAA, they said we were not cooperating, but we had turned over all information to the attorney by the specified deadline and there were emails to show that the deadline was met on our side. They were furious that we got no response from our phone carrier after turning in numerous text log requests through the company channels. In talking with an in- store employee of the carrier, I found out that requests for those logs usually go unanswered unless a subpoena is involved because of the amount of printing and shipping it would cost the company. So although we made 4 separate requests the text message logs were never received. This process of back and forth, bullying, and threats of not complying goes on for months.

News trucks parked in front of my home, reporters knocking on my front door and fans of rival fan bases vandalizing my home was my state of existence for months. My child was continually being vilified as a thug and a gangster. All of this is swirling, and there is no statement made by the university to stop the blows that are being handed to us. We felt good about being made to pay back money for the rental and moving on, but it was leaked that we were lying to the NCAA. Who leaked it I don't know, but for certain somebody was sharing confidential information from the investigation with the media.

My son was never ruled ineligible to play by the NCAA. The university decided not to play him for fear of the NCAA lodging a formal investigation and delving deeper into the program. In December 2013 I was called into Coach Williams's office and told that the decision had been made by the university to not submit papers to the NCAA for reinstatement. Conveniently the decision was made after completion of the fall semester was completed. Without passing grades from my son that semester there would have been NCAA sanctions due to Academic Progress Rate (APR) issues. We knew days before anyone else knew. I demanded to meet with the AD to hear the explanation why they would not allow the NCAA to make a ruling. The answer I received made me very aware of what I had heard so many times before. The name on the front of your college jersey will always be more important than the name on the back. There was too much information that would come out if the reinstatement papers were filed and that they didn't want to put him through any more. For seven months my son was dragged through the media, he still went to class and he, by admission of his coach, was the best teammate he could be while waiting on the process. How could anything in the paperwork make it any worse for him? The things he had done were already leaked to the press. I found out that my son was breaking the rules, and I dealt with that as the entire sports world watched; remaining silent while people gossiped and laughed behind my back. Scared that if I said anything the NCAA would punish him more severely and I didn't want to do anything to hurt the university. I will not say that I blame the university because if the paperwork was submitted it would be accessible through public records request and what would have been revealed were more names of players connected to the rental cars and parking violations. Although, my son had given the NCAA the path in to investigate through his actions that summer that opened Pandora's Box, but I knew he did not place the full content in that box alone. My son took the blame for everything that he did and never tried to involve anyone else in his mistakes and because he would not name other teammates he was labeled as a liar. He wasn't a liar; he merely refused to implicate anyone else in his NCAA interviews, when others interviewed were happy to name him. He took the full punishment of his coach, which was outlined as to what his punishment would be if he chose to stay and fight to get back. In the end, he was dismissed from the university and the AD felt good about the decision he had made because as he said, "Let's face it he was going to leave early for the NBA anyway."

I can still see the pictures the media circulated for months on him sitting in his suit all alone on UNC's bench during the Texas game. Everyone during that game was still speculating on his return, but that picture did not show a young man that was still waiting for his final punishment. It showed a young man at his lowest point, knowing that he

65

would never wear his uniform again. Knowing that before that game the decision by the university had already been made not to submit his paperwork to the NCAA. I watched that game knowing that the weight of the world lay squarely on his shoulders, and that I had to pull it together to make sure he didn't shatter into a million pieces. From this experience, I learned that when you are on top everybody loves you and when you make a mistake and fall from grace those same people singing your praises will help dig the hole to bury you. I learned that the Carolina Way is not something that is fully understood by those from the outside because the true way of family is to stick by you until the bitter end and not release you as a sacrifice. I learned that sometimes your children make mistakes and fall into the wrong crowd no matter how much you try to guide them in the right direction. I learned that as much as a school covets your child in the recruiting process and promises to watch them just like you would they too can allow things to fall through the cracks not paying attention to the signs. The most important thing that I learned is that God's plan is always the right plan and cannot be questioned. A weaker person would have been broken and allowed their child to give up. My son dealt with his consequences with his head held high and because of that he is still part of the true Carolina family and I still consider Roy Williams a friend. God's plan for his life was not how we thought it would be, but something very different. God's path for my son was not what I planned, not what man had planned, but what God planned. And all the struggles I had gone through prepared me to be his rock and help him through that tumultuous time in his life.

Chapter 8

The Game Changer

In 2014 after a journey through the D- League my son saw his dream realized on June 26, 2014, his name was called as the 26th overall pick in the NBA Draft. He made history becoming the first D- League player to ever be drafted in the 1st round of the NBA draft. The next morning he was headed to Charlotte, NC to play for the Hornets. In that moment, it became apparent I had poured everything I had into making sure my son was ok, but now I was left alone with no companionship, and I knew it was time to find a mate. Now read this line very carefully...I decided it was time for ME to find a mate. Over the course of the next year, I found out that picking someone myself was just a disaster waiting to happen. The guy I started dating said all the right things; however, he was saying all those things to his wife as well. That's right the guy I chose was still married and played the both of us using his job and travel as a way to spend time with me and as his way of being able to be home with his wife and two young children. It took me some time to grasp that he was a manipulating liar, but after a few weeks of some real self-reflection, I realized one thing. This man was who I had chosen and not one time did I think to allow God to move. I had let a handsome face and a bought of loneliness defeat me. I had learned to trust in God I knew his power, but yet again I was doing things on my own without his direction, and the outcome was exactly how it should have been for not being obedient. I prayed and told God that the next man in my life would be exactly who he chose for me.

In December of 2014, I exchanged numbers with one of my son's teammate's father. I needed extra tickets to the Christmas tournament, and he had an extra one for me. We met at the game, and he gave me the ticket. With a huge smile on his face he said, "Don't you look beautiful tonight Ma." From that game on he always had something to say to me, and most of the time it was like we were in elementary school because he was always picking on me. I remember one game I went to I had to come straight from work. I had been at the General Assembly all day so I was exhausted. I was dressed in a black suit with my heels still on. Of course, when I took my seat there he was with that big smile he always had. He looked at me and said, "Who died and I'm sorry for your loss." I just looked at him and said to myself this damn smart aleck gets on my last nerve. I proceeded to tell him that nobody had died, that I was coming from work. He just smiled his huge grin and said ok. As the season progressed, we would talk often about the game and the kids. We became what I would call civil. I talked to him like I did some of the other parents on the team.

One Sunday he came by my house to pick up my son to head to a basketball game with him and his son. I had gone out to a movie with a friend and we were inside the house talking when he stopped by. After my friend left to head home, I was laying on my couch watching TV when I received a text message that said, "I am jealous, wish I could be hanging out with you." The school season had ended, so it had been a while since I had seen or talked to him. My response was simply, "Sorry." A week or so after that his son was at my house with my son. They both started asking if I had gotten a text from his dad. I told them I had. They asked what I thought about his dad. I told them his dad was funny but a bit of an asshole. Then the big question was popped, "Why don't you go out on a date with him?" I must say the question threw me for a loop. I had heard stories from other people about his dad, and I was sure that I was not the type of woman that he wanted to date. I also had made a covenant with God that the next man I was involved with would be sent by him. The funny thing is I could faintly hear that voice saying give him a chance. So, I told the boys that if he wanted to go out with me, then he needed to ask. I was not about to ask him out. The next day my phone rang, and I saw his name on my caller ID. I was hesitant but picked up on about the 4th ring. It was him, and I could literally hear his smile through the phone. We talked for a while and oddly enough it was a pleasant conversation. He asked if I was going to the basketball tournament with the boys on the following weekend and I told him that I was. His response was great maybe we can go out while we are there. I thought why not so I said ok. Over the next week, we talked on the phone every day, and I couldn't remember laughing so much in a long time. My initial thoughts of him were being changed because getting to know him was easy and he was actually quite charming. When I arrived in Hampton, I called and let him know I had made it safely. He had gotten into town a bit later in the afternoon than I did. That night I hung out with some girlfriends at my son's game and called him afterward. I drove to meet him at his hotel. When I got there, we headed out to grab a bite to eat. We ended up at this little bar where we sat for hours. We laughed and talked about everything from sports to us both growing up in little country towns with farm animals. We had so much in common it was almost scary. That night was truly the best date of my life. When I saw him at the game the next day, his smile met me from across the gym when I walked in. I didn't sit next to him, and he looked confused. After the game, he was standing at the bottom of the bleachers and held out his hand to help me down. He actually made me blush with his coy gentlemanly like behavior. After that weekend I knew that something very special was about to happen, but I wasn't going to rush it. For weeks we dated and never said anything to our children. I think we both wanted to make sure that what we were feeling was real.

One day we talked, and he looked at me and said, "Do you believe in God?" I shared with him some intimate details about my past, my struggle with loving God, and my triumph in owning who I was and getting back to loving God again. He looked at me and was quite for a long time. He then said to me, "I just gave my life to Christ a few months ago, and I'm working on being a better man." In that instant, I knew that God had placed this man in my life. A man that I never would have chosen on my own, because he was way too cocky and obnoxious for me and he got on my nerves like nobody I had ever met before. After getting to know him and finding it so easy to share my past and him being an open book about his past and mistakes that he had made it turned out he was not who his book cover made him appear to be. He was a man striving to do better and be better. He was the man God had sent me. Our relationship was revealed and it was not all smooth sailing. There were some people that were angry that we had connected and spoke demise over our relationship. I was called names- desperate, fake, the devil, etc. - and defamed because I was with him. There were those that thought because I was financially stable with a son in the NBA and he was rebuilding that he was only with me because I had money. We both knew what God was ordering for our lives, and we followed in his path regardless of the negativity and nastiness that swirled around about our relationship.

When the high school basketball season ended he had moved back to Atlanta. He was back and forth from Georgia to North Carolina to see his son and me. We took our first road trip together, and I was excited like a little kid. He picked me up from the hair salon and my stylist said to me, "You really like him don't you?" That weekend trip to his hometown I visited with his friends and family. I learned that he was a legend in his hometown. He was the high school basketball star and a musical prodigy. The people in his small hometown welcomed me with open arms and reminded me of what small town love felt like. I fell in love with Spanish moss in Charleston, SC that weekend and I fell in love with him too. Over several months my children had grown to love him just as I had. It became clear one day when he was visiting that being apart was not going to work for us. That day we sat on the patio and laughed and talked for hours. He was helping me with some things around the house, and the next thing on the list was to clean out my fire pit. He lifted the cover top, and a bird flew out! As he got ready to burn the rubbish that was inside the pit, we noticed a bird's nest. He was so protective of the nest and the baby blue speckled eggs inside of it. He placed the nest of eggs on a tree limb by the back gate. He looked at me and said, "The baby birds need protecting until their mom comes back." In that instant, I could feel his love for family, and I knew that one day I would marry this man. A few weeks following we moved in together. He found a job and things were turning around for him financially. He was adamant that if we were going to live together we needed to be thinking about a lifetime together. He was not interested in just living together he wanted a life together. Months passed and he showed me that he was committed to spending his life with me.

It was Thanksgiving, and I was spending it with him and his entire family for the first time. I had a great time laughing, eating, and enjoying getting to know his family even better. My boys were in NC where they spend Thanksgiving with their dad and his family every year, but they knew I was getting a major surprise on Thanksgiving. During dinner, he stood up and called everyone's attention to the front of the room. He started talking about his cousin who had just graduated from culinary school. Everyone was so proud of her and her mom had a big party planned for the next night. It was only fitting that her big cuz would talk about her accomplishment. I sat on the couch and listened to him and was checking out my social media too. Then all of a sudden, the tone of the speech changed, and he called his oldest son to the front of the room. He handed his dad a red box. He started to talk about how God had blessed him and that he wanted to do something he had never did before in front of his entire family. He stood right in front of me with the red box. I could not hold back the tears. He got down on one knee and said, "Will you be my husband....I mean my wife?!" He was so nervous and tears streamed down my face as I looked at him. I said yes because this man was who God sent me. This man was exactly who God knew I would spend the rest of my life with. This man had filled a place in my heart that for many years was always hollow. This man treated me with the warmth, love, and kindness that all women should feel from their mate. This man was my forever, and I had allowed God to choose him for me. We celebrated into the early morning with family and God showed me that this is what real love is. Ordained by God and equally yoked to build a life of love, friendship, and forever. My life had come full circle in that moment. I had been freed of all the wrongs in my past. I had been given the final piece to the puzzle of my life that I had tried so hard to make for myself. This beautiful creation made by God was now a reality, and the love of God had never been more apparent in my life.

Chapter 9

Why People Need YOU

Your voice is given to you by God. It is uniquely yours, and through it you can make an indelible mark on this world. There are things in your life that you will experience that will cause you to allow your voice to be altered in different ways. Your job is to take those experiences in stride and not allow them to take your voice away. For many years I allowed my pain to take away my voice. I lived in the shadows of self-hate, depression, and defeat. Experiences in this world have different effects on each person, but you control the effect that it has from the moment you encounter the experience. The only way you can keep your voice intact is to fight. Most people are taught right and wrong and even if they are not they have the innate human ability to know right from wrong. Your job on this earth is to find that good inside yourself and use it as good.

As a young girl being molested by my father, I knew that what was happening to me was not right. I allowed the fear of him hurting me and fear of my mom being angry at me to take away my voice. I endured years of abuse until I owned what was happening to me was wrong and I fought back. The sexual abuse stopped, and the verbal abuse strangled me. I allowed the words; ugly, too tall, whore, big lips, black, bitch and other negative words to shape my self-image. I allowed the hurt from those words to push me into doing things to make them untrue. In my hurt I knew right from wrong. I knew I was not raised to be on pole twerking for dollar bills, but I allowed my voice to be lost. I allowed the thrill of getting money mask the words that shaped my self-worth. It took me looking at myself in a mirror and learning to love my dark skin, tall frame, and big lips to take back control of my life.

People like me and others who suffered through abuse, depression, self-loathing and shame are needed in this world. The world has plenty of perfect people that set goals and follow through and have no bumps in the road. They live what is considered the good and normal life. The people who live life through knock down blows and broken promises are the people that rise from the ashes like a Phoenix and set the world on fire. Trials and tribulations are the things that build character and resiliency. The tests and burdens that seem to be the most perilous situations in your life are the foundations of picturesque statues that are admired by the world. The laughs and gossip from people cheering for your demise are the words that should be internalized to motivate you to create artistic masterpieces that are read and accepted by the world as powerful creations of empowerment. My grandma used to always say, "God don't create mess so get in line and be who he created." She knew I would find my way and probably knew I would remember and use her powerful one- liner.

There are six things or steps that I want to share that will help you to work yourself out of being mentally stuck. These things redirected my life and I believe will help you to redirect yours.

1. Look in the mirror and identify what the most painful thing in your life has been and tackle it head

on. Don't allow that one pivotal tragedy in your life to define who you will be. One of the greatest challenges in your life will be owning who you are, who you have been, and then allowing yourself to live in happiness and peace with what you have found and accepted. Living life according to your own truth and your own terms mean. It has to make sense to you and you have to make peace with it in your own way. There are no do- overs in life. You must accept the journey and embrace the lessons it has taught. No matter how painful or embarrassing; your truth creates who you are.

2. Say out loud to yourself or someone all of the things that you have done in your life to yourself or to other people that were destructive and say out loud that you are sorry. Not only are you apologizing to others but you are apologizing to yourself. Allowing your own truth to be revealed and forgiving yourself. You cannot allow other people to define who you should be. You are uniquely who you are and if it doesn't meet the standards of others it does not make them right and you wrong; it merely makes you different. The only relationship that you need to make sure is in order is your relationship with God. Your path doesn't need to make sense to anyone but God!

3. Don't hold on to grudges. If someone has hurt you and you can't find closure from that pain you can't allow that pain to control you and weigh you down. The journey and the choices that you have made in

your life will not be understood by everyone. Remember that you are here to live the one life that you have been given and owning your truth is not meant to be understood by everyone. Living life according to your own truth and your own terms is not meant to devalue others, but meant to empower you to be fearless in the face of your past. Owning your truth does not mean that you are defiant to order and a moral compass. It simply means that you have identified who you are and learned to live in that truth. Owning your truth is about not just being comfortable in the skin of your past but the skin of your future and allowing your truth to help others.

4. Find out what your passion is. Don't go through life marking time with nothing that energizes your entire soul. Find that thing that you feel good about and makes you want to share it with the world. Your passion is what gives you a pulse it stimulates your heart and your mind. Passion is often a scary thing because it means that you are dreaming of what could be and not what is. Passion requires you to often step out on faith. Passion requires you to jump without knowing exactly where you will land. Passion is your journey to finding out exactly what God put you on this earth to be. Passion is allowing your story to be used to edify. Passion is knowing what it feels like to be a change agent and walking firmly in that gift God has given you.

5. Always tell the truth even if it is not the popular thing to do or say. It will free your conscious of any baggage that you should not carry. Often times being honest is hard because the truth may hurt, but your ability to value truth will be a freeing tool to master in owning your truth and helping other to own theirs. When you lie, you continue to allow situations and circumstances to exist in your future. Telling the truth makes those situations or circumstance a part of your past. Telling the truth makes you vulnerable to people's reactions, but it allows you to move on free of guilt. Telling the truth will often times uncover the lies of others, but be steadfast in your own truth in hopes that your truth will bring others to their truth as well.

6. Love God more than you love yourself. Allow God to move you in the sequence that he has planned for your life. Accept that all things, good and bad, are the threads woven by God's hand to create the beautiful tapestry that makes you who you are. Allow your authentic being to exist and be happy with it. The love of God is an all-encompassing feeling. He picks you up when you are down. He cheers for you in your victory. He chastises you in your disobedience. Learning to love God first and above all else is a humbling existence, but the rewards of that love are overwhelming. The book of first Perter 5:6 says, "Humble yourselves therefore, under the mighty hand of God so that at the proper time he may exalt you."

People that have been given what some will call a tough journey are God's toughest soldiers. People that have gone to battle are needed. We were not put here to suffer and be defeated. We were put here to show the power of God and the works he can make in lives of those willing to follow him. No matter how hard we fight to not be those vessels, it is God's plan to have us on the ground fighting his battle. You are needed, and the first step in finding out what God has in store for you is owning the truth and the accepting the special gift you have been given by God. Until I accepted that my hardships were not punishments, but God's blessings to create his solider I was lost. Now that I have accepted his plan it is abundantly clear that people need me and my job is to help others see why they are needed too.

Chapter 10

Own Your Truth

Domestic violence can have an ingrained impact on every facet of your life. It is up to you the steps that you take to be in control of your life and to accept the journey that your life has taken you on. It is not always easy to look in the mirror and say I was sexually molested, I was an alcoholic, I was addicted to drugs, I was a stripper, I was a liar, and a user. After admitting your truth to yourself, it is even harder to tell those things to others. When you ask God to order your steps, you must be obedient in following the path that he lays before you. The things that I have revealed in this book are my truth, and God planned for my truth to be told. The things that we experience shape our definition of who we are. The truth is; the power that others hold over you is much stronger than your will to overcome on your own, which is why step number 6 is so important. The love of God is the power that can overcome it all. The love of God is the only thing that pulled me out of the darkness and chaos in my life. The love of God released the chains that held me down from getting on the path he designed. The love of God is the only thing that makes me strong enough to own my truth and tell my truth because that truth will help someone dealing with the weight of the world holding them down.

Whatever it is that you were is in your past you have to accept that truth and move forward. You must decide to take a different path. You hold the power to allow your life's journey to empower you and to use that journey to empower others. You also have to accept that everyone will not appreciate your journey and there will be some that will still condemn you for your past transgressions. I know that some people will read this book and decide to use it as a weapon against my character. Some people will use my truth to pick on my children about what I used to be. I know that they are prepared because God's soldiers are always ready for battle. They have been taught to value and respect people for everything that they are. But, when you are able to own your truth you know what your purpose is and why God has led you on your new journey. No matter what your past holds and no matter how broken you have been the key to finding your way and turning things around is to own your truth and live your life according to that truth on your own terms! You can't allow man and the fear of shame to change your direction. Even as I wrote this book I asked myself several times did I really want everyone to read this book and know my inner most secrets? Did I want my children to have to face the ridicule of what would be revealed? Did I want to subject my fiancé to everyone knowing the details of my past? Then as always that voice spoke to me and clarified that this book was not about me and it's not about how those that love me unconditionally would deal with the truth being told. This book was his plan and his design. This book validates the obstacles and hurdles in my path as part of my journey to get to where his plan was designed to send me. This book was about helping others and using my truth to illustrate his power to transform lives. This book was always meant to be written because he gave one of his toughest battles to one of his strongest soldiers and my fight was designed to help others. The journey to a transformative life cannot be taken successfully walking alone. A relationship with God has to be incorporated into the task of overcoming.

I share things out loud that were once the very things that held me in shackles living ashamed of what my truth would make people think of me. Could Entice ever overcome where she had been? Would I ever be able to gain credibility knowing that I had been an avid drug user? If I tried to move up the corporate ladder would my past hold me back? Would sharing my story cause me to lose the love and respect of my children? Again, all those questions were in the forefront of my mind, but I decided that I would not be defined by my past and I would not allow my past to paralyze my life and take away my voice. I realized my potential, and I found my way back to how I was raised. I found my way back to God and his voice became so clear once I laid my burdens down. I realize God's reasons for my journey every day when things happen to people that I know and love God gives me the ability to be the strong one or be the shoulder to lean on. I know now that God took me through the things that I went through because his plan for my life was to speak life, his plan for my life was to tell the people that you can do all things through Christ that strengthens you! Don't give up on God because he will never give up on you!

In Proverbs 3:5-6 it says, "Trust in the LORD with all your heart, and do not lean on your own understanding. In all your ways acknowledge him, and he will make straight your paths." I believe that God makes no mistakes for he is

Alpha and Omega, the beginning and the end and he holds all power in his hands. I implore you to read deep into the story of my life and find something that speaks to you in your situation. Use the words that you have read to plant a seed that will grow into foliage of hope and aspirations for success. The only way to live in your purpose is to own it and do it on your own terms.

Domestic Violence Statistics

Every community is impacted by domestic violence. It affects every class of people regardless of age, gender, race, sexual orientation, religion, or socioeconomic status. Physical violence is more than always partnered with verbal and emotional abuse. Victims of domestic violence suffer from the perils of stalking, control and clear patterns of abuse. Victims suffer from physical violation, mental manipulation, and some even death. Domestic violence is often a multi-generational issue with lifetime cycles of abuse.

The statistics shared below should not be taken lightly. If you or someone you know is struggling with domestic violence, please contact the national hotline for help 1-800-799-7233.

1-800-787-3224 (TTY for Deaf/hard of hearing). You are not alone and there is help to remove you from the threat of physical harm.

- One in three girls and at least one in seven boys are sexually molested before the age of 18. (Ramsey)
- Between 75 and 90 % of the time, the abuser is an adult that the child knows.(Ramsey)
- Sexual abuse in the family is likely to begin when the child is as young as 3-6 years of age and, if unreported, continues into adolescence.(Ramsey)
- In this country, a daughter is molested by her father every 30 minutes.(Ramsey)

- **Guilt, shame, and blame**. You might feel guilty about not having been able to stop the abuse, or even blame yourself if you experienced physical pleasure. It is important for you to understand that it was the person that hurt you that should be held accountable—not you.(Adult Survivors of Child Abuse)

- **Self-esteem**. You may struggle with low self-esteem, which can be a result of the negative messages you received from your abuser(s), and from having your personal safety violated or ignored. Low self-esteem can affect many different areas of your life such as your relationships, your career, and even your health.(Adult Survivors of Child Abuse)

References

Adult Survivors of Child Abuse. (n.d.). Retrieved September 7, 2016

Ramsey, J. S. (Ed.). (1998). *Telling the Truth: Preaching about Sexual and Domestic Violence.* Cleveland: United Church Press.

About the Author

Wendy is a graduate of Guilford College with a BS in Criminal Justice. She holds a Master's in Public Administration. Previously, Wendy served as Chief Operating Officer for A United Community, LLC, where she created and implemented organizational strategies, policies, and practices. She is currently a registered state lobbyist for the Winston-Salem Chamber of Commerce. Wendy advocates and secures funding and legislative support for priority projects in a dynamic, ever-changing political environment.

Wendy serves on the Board of Visitors for Guilford College; appointed by the President of the University of NC System to the Center for Design Innovation Advisory Board; Leadership Winston-Salem Board of Directors, Program Council, and Human Relations Committee.

Wendy is a singer, motivational speaker, and certified adversity life coach. Wendy has three sons PJ, 24; Tre, 16; and Walter 12.

Made in the USA
Columbia, SC
07 February 2018